Introduction

This book is a reference guide for guitarists. It is not intended as a method book, but rather as a reference book of scales that are easily accessible to the beginner or advanced guitarist. Regardless of your musical interest, this book contains the majority of scales you will encounter in most styles of music (rock, jazz, country, or blues). Strong scale knowledge will help build familiarity with the fretboard and help develop technical ability. The thirteen scales covered in this book are:

- **major (Ionian)**
- **natural minor (Aeolian)**
- **Dorian**
- **Phrygian**
- **Lydian**
- **Mixolydian**
- **Locrian**
- **Harmonic minor**
- **Whole tone**
- **Diminished (whole-half)**
- **Pentatonic (major)**
- **Pentatonic (minor)**
- **Blues scale (with major third and flattened fifth)**

Although there are many more scales available, these scale types were chosen for their popularity as well as their usefulness. *The Little Black Book Of Scales* has been designed with the player in mind. You don't have to go to your bookshelf to find that bulky chord encyclopedia that your music stand can't even hold up, and it doesn't take up all the space on your music stand. It is easy-to-carry and easy-to-use. We hope that this book will serve as a valuable reference source during your years as a developing guitarist.

How to use this book

It is strongly recommended that you develop a practice
regimen in which you devote some time to scale study.
If you practice one hour each session, then devote fifteen or
twenty minutes to scale study. Another approach would be
to practice your warm-up exercises with a different scale
each day.

Here are some helpful tips:

* At the top of each page you will find the scale type
and below you'll find the scale formula
(W = whole-step and H = half-step).

* Notice that there are five suggested scale types along
with their fingerings. (The scale types and fingerings are
only suggested guidelines; you are encouraged to develop
your own scale types and fingerings).

* The scales are written in both standard notation and
tablature. You will find a fretboard diagram at the bottom of
the page displaying the scale pattern (the root of the scale
appears as a circle while the other scale tones appear as
black dots).

* In addition, the five fingering types are bracketed at the
top of the fretboard diagram to help you visualize the scale
pattern all over the neck.

For more tips on how scales can help you progress
as a soloist, see the Solos and Scales section on page 296.

Whether you are looking to develop chops (technique)
or broaden your scale vocabulary, *The Little Black Book Of
Scales* is for you.

C Major (Ionian)

WWHWWWH

Type 1

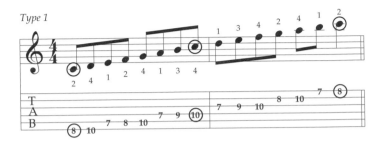

Type 2

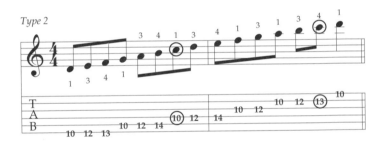

Type 3

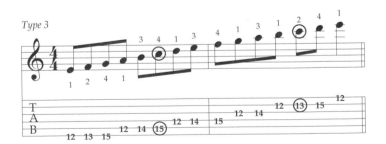

8

Type 4

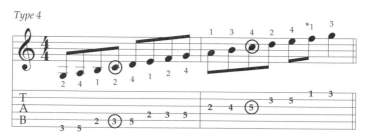

* position shift

Type 5

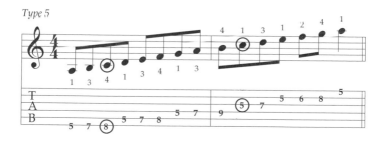

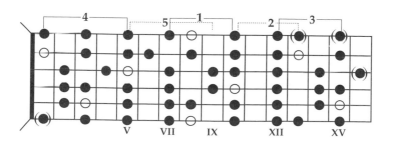

C Natural Minor (Aeolian)

WHWWHWW

Type 1

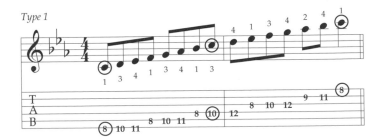

Type 2

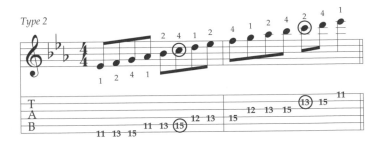

Type 3

10

Type 4

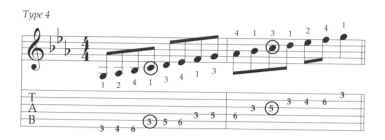

Type 5

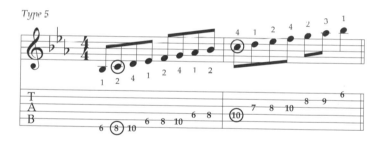

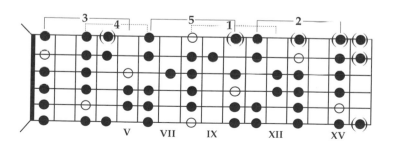

11

C Dorian

WHWWWHW

Type 1

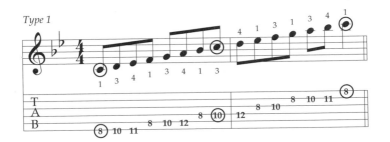

Type 2

Type 3

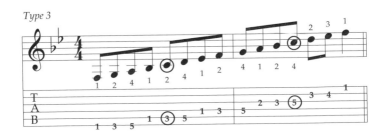

Type 4

Type 5

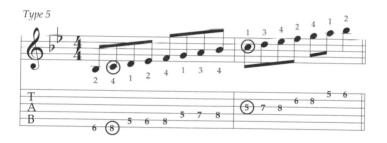

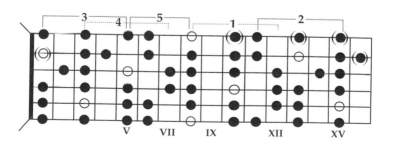

C Phrygian

HWWWHWW

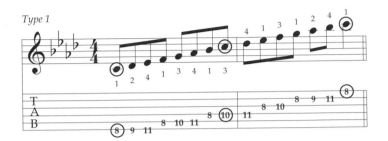

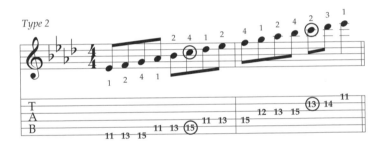

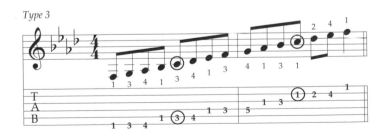

14

Type 4

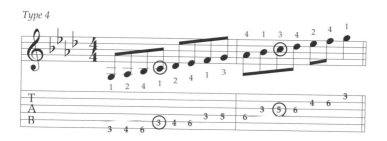

Type 5

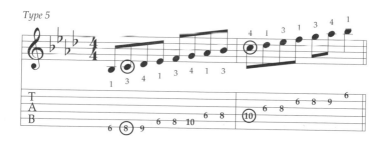

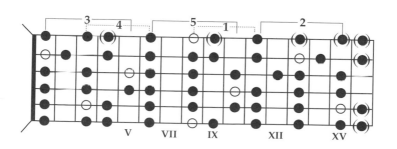

15

C Lydian

WWWHWWH

Type 1

Type 2

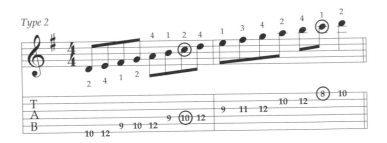

Type 3

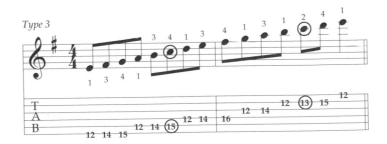

Type 4

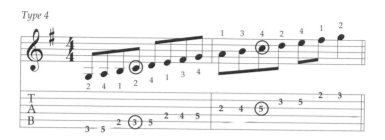

Type 5

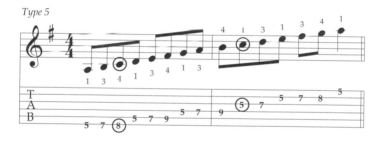

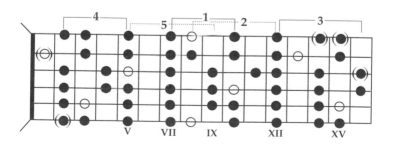

17

C Mixolydian

WWHWWHW

Type 1

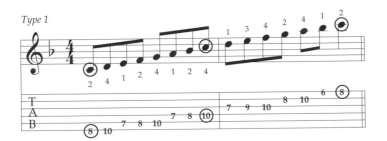

Type 2

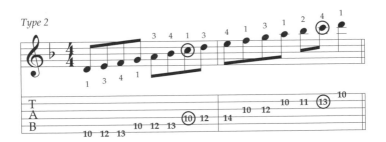

Type 3

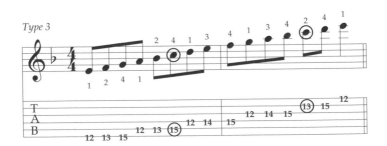

18

Type 4

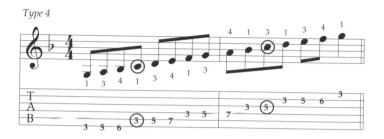

Type 5

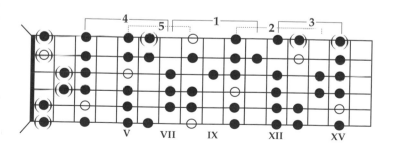

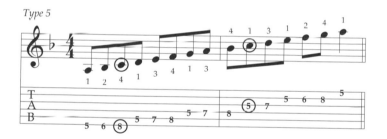

C Locrian

HWWHWWW

Type 1

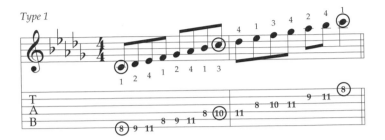

Type 2

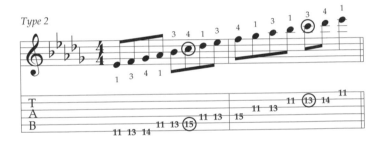

Type 3

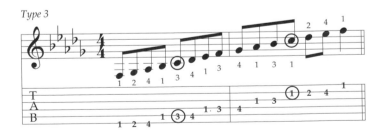

20

Type 4

Type 5

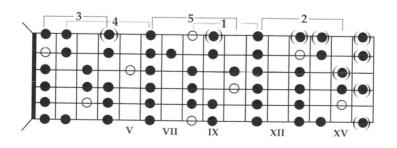

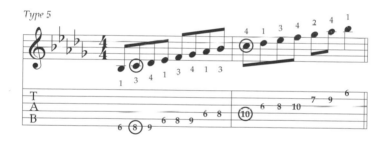

21

C Harmonic Minor

WHWWHm3H

Type 1

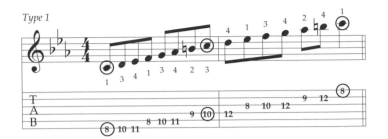

Type 2

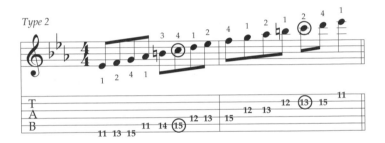

Type 3

position shift

Type 4

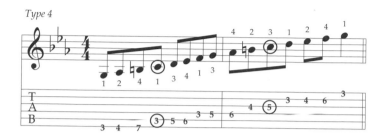

Type 5

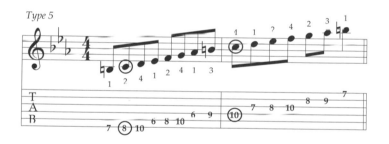

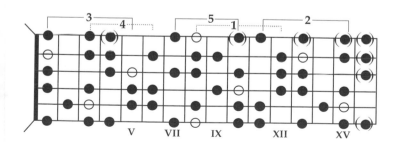

C Whole Tone

WWWWWW

Type 1

Type 2

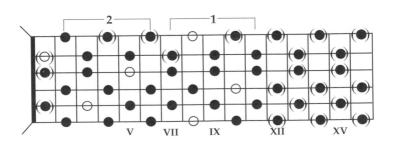

C Diminished (whole-half)

WHWHWHWH

Type 1

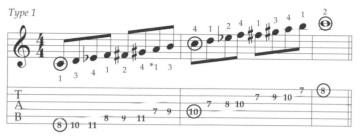

* *position shift*

Type 2

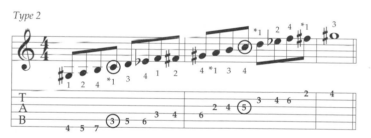

* *position shift*

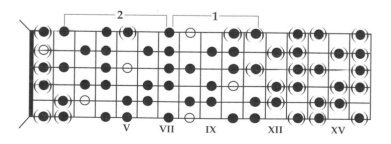

C Pentatonic (Major)

WWm3Wm3

Type 1

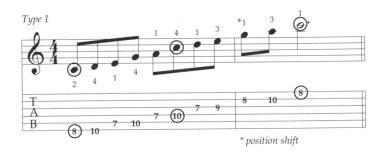

* position shift

Type 2

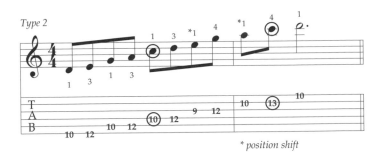

* position shift

Type 3

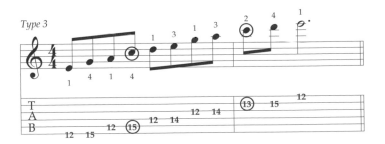

Type 4

* position shift

Type 5

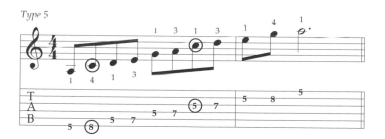

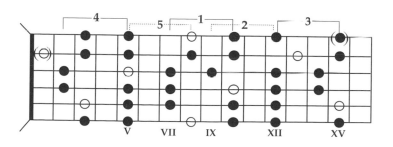

27

C Pentatonic (Minor)

m3WWm3W

Type 1

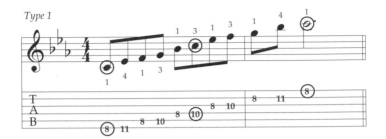

Type 2

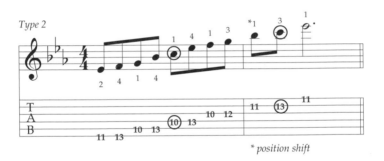

* position shift

Type 3

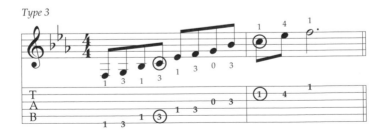

Type 4

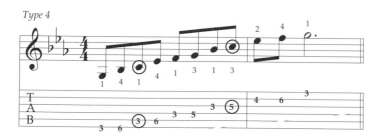

Type 5

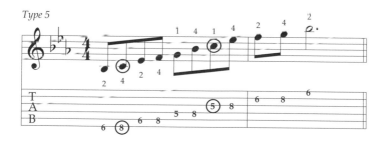

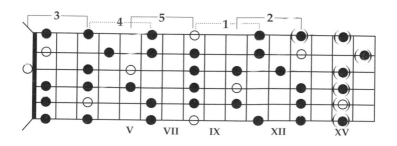

29

C Blues Scale
(with major 3rd & flattened 5th)

m3HHHHm3W

Type 1

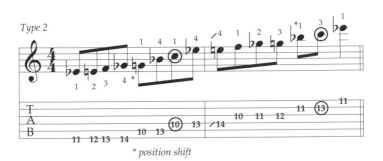

* position shift

Type 2

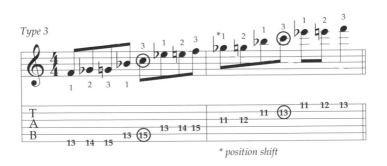

* position shift

Type 3

* position shift

Type 4

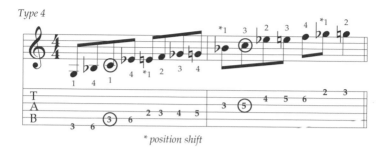

* position shift

Type 5

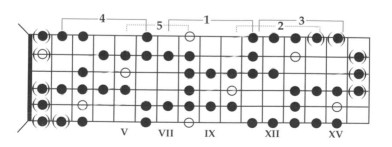

* position shift

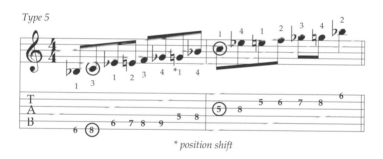

31

D♭ Major (Ionian)

WWHWWWH

Type 1

Type 2

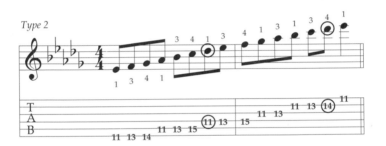

Type 3

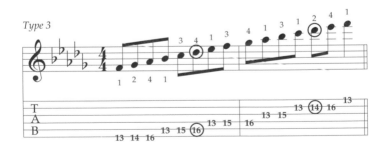

Type 4

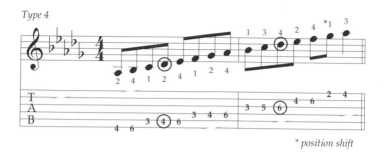

* position shift

Type 5

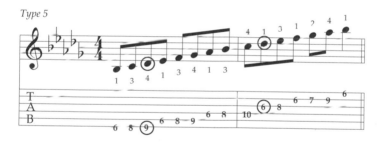

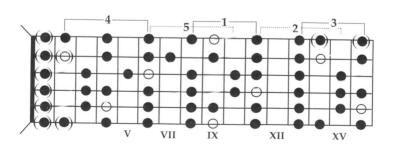

D♭ Natural Minor (Aeolian)

WHWWHWW

Type 1

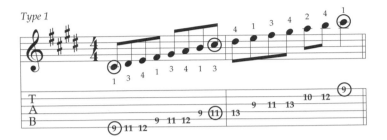

Type 2

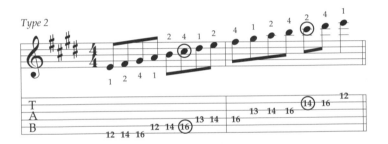

Type 3

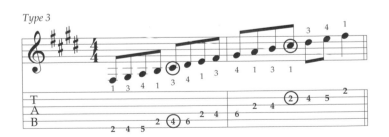

34

Type 4

Type 5

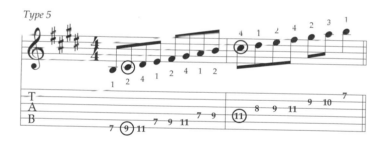

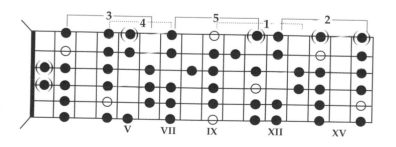

35

D♭ Dorian

WHWWWHW

Type 1

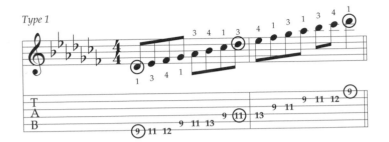

Type 2

Type 3

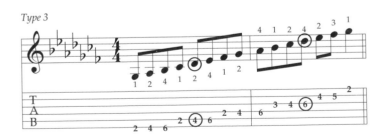

Type 4

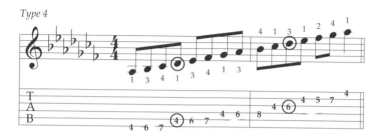

Type 5

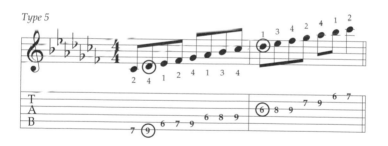

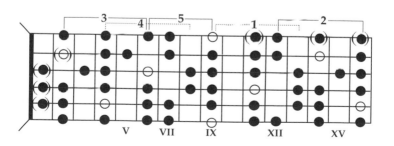

D♭ Phrygian

HWWWHWW

Type 1

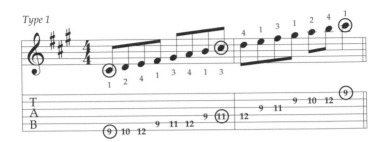

Type 2

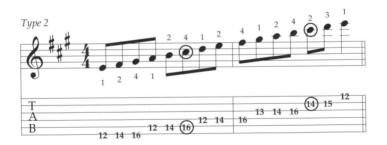

Type 3

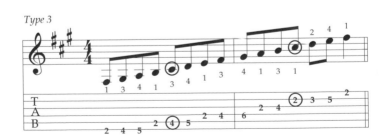

Type 4

Type 5

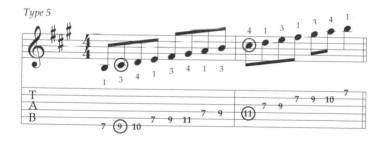

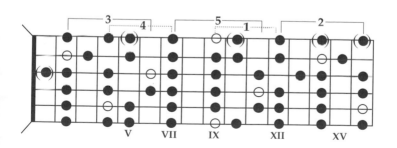

39

D♭ Lydian

WWWHWWH

Type 1

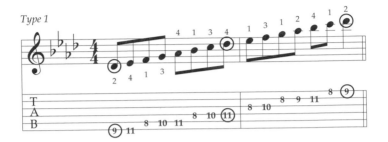

Type 2

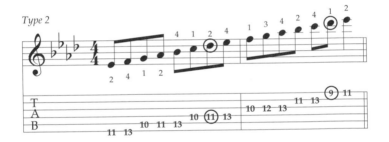

Type 3

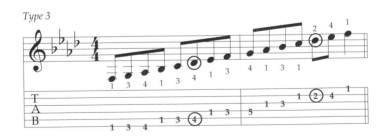

Type 4

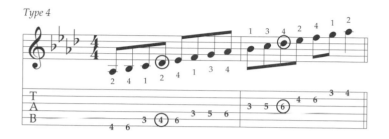

Type 5

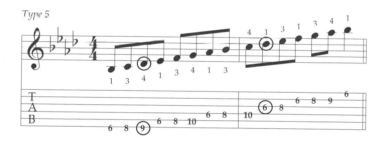

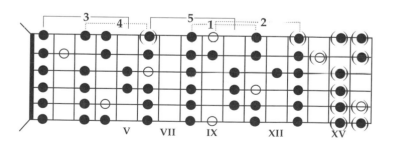

41

D♭ Mixolydian

WWHWWHW

Type 1

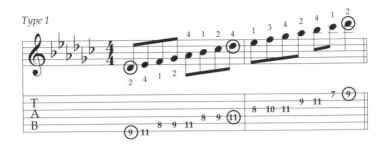

Type 2

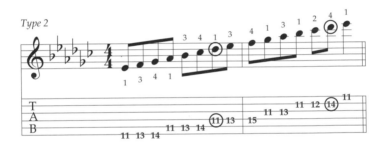

Type 3

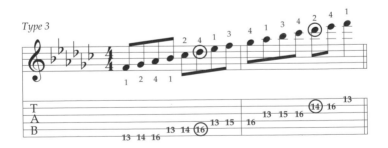

42

Type 4

Type 5

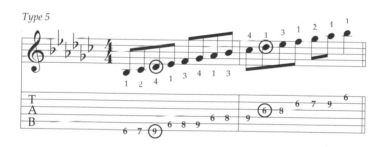

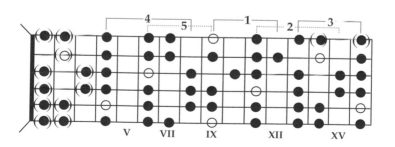

43

D♭ Locrian

HWWHWWW

Type 1

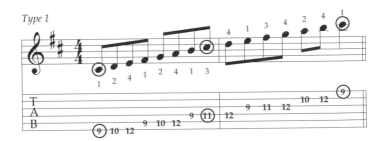

Type 2

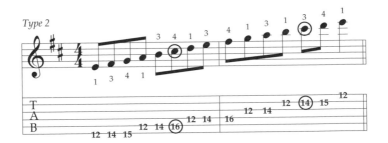

Type 3

Type 4

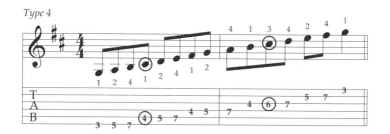

Type 5

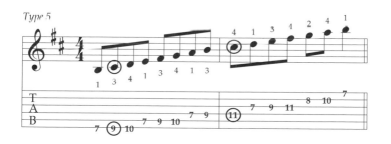

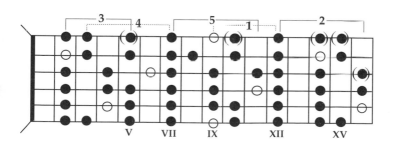

45

D♭ Harmonic Minor

WHWWHm3H

Type 1

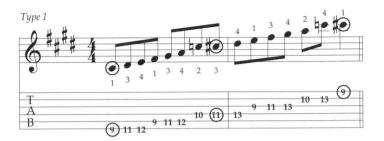

Type 2

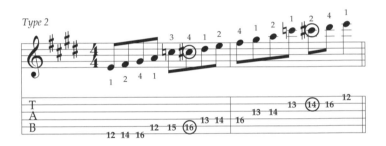

Type 3

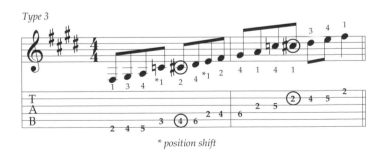

* position shift

46

Type 4

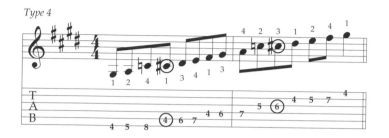

Type 5

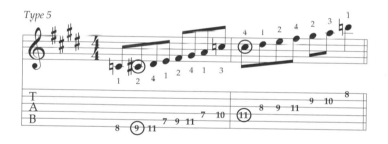

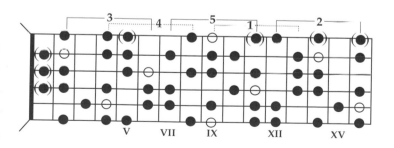

47

D♭ Whole Tone

wwwwww

Type 1

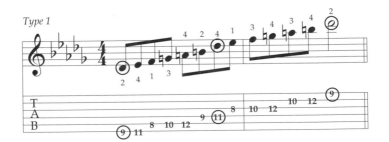

Type 2

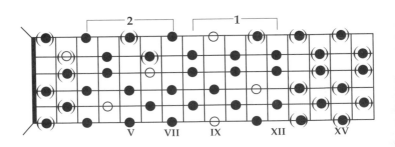

48

D♭ Diminished (whole-half)

WHWHWHWH

Type 1

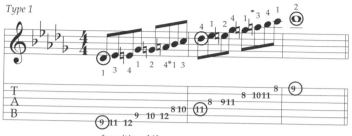

* position shift

Type 2

* position shift

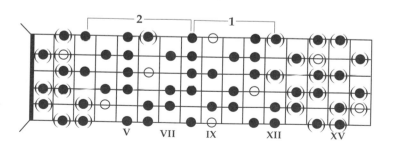

49

D♭ Pentatonic (Major)

WWm3Wm3

Type 1

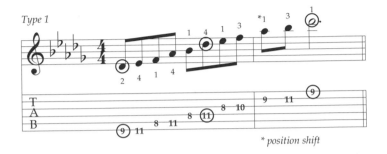

* position shift

Type 2

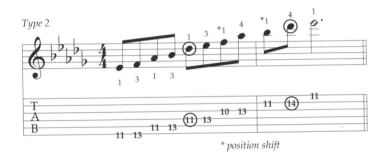

* position shift

Type 3

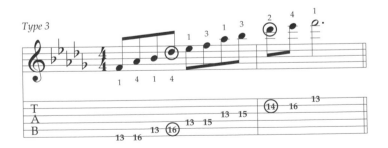

Type 4

* position shift

Type 5

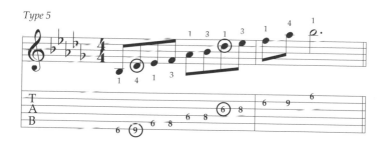

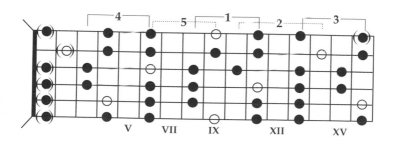

51

D♭ Pentatonic (Minor)

m3WWm3W

Type 1

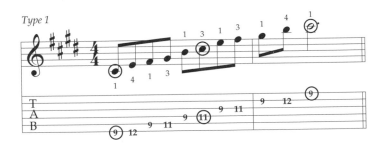

Type 2

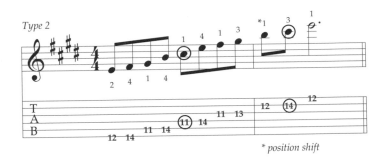

* position shift

Type 3

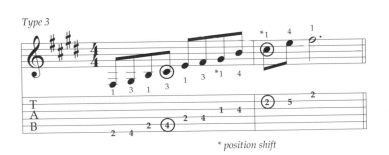

* position shift

52

Type 4

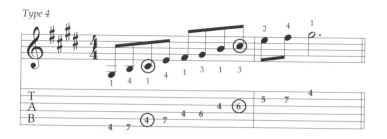

Type 5

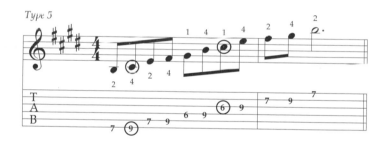

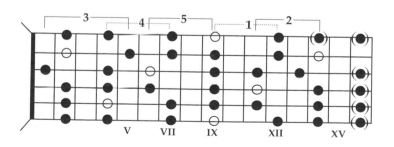

53

D♭ Blues Scale
(with major 3rd & flattened 5th)

m3HHHHm3W

Type 1

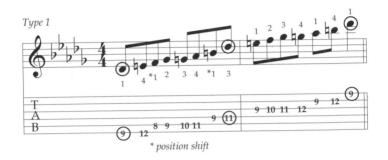

* position shift

Type 2

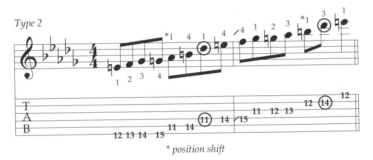

* position shift

Type 3

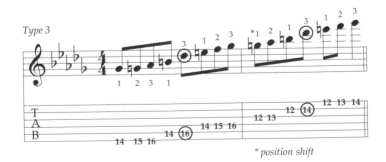

* position shift

54

Type 4

* position shift

Type 5

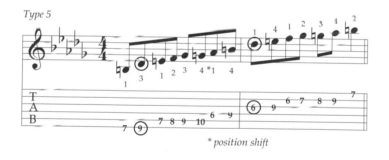

* position shift

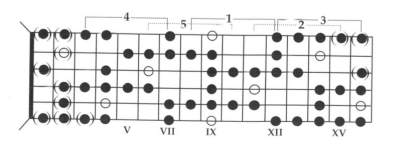

55

D Major (Ionian)

WWHWWWH

Type 1

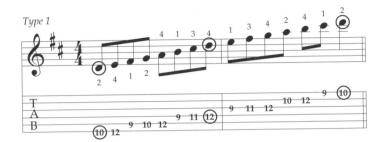

Type 2

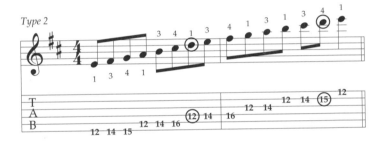

Type 3

Type 4

* position shift

Type 5

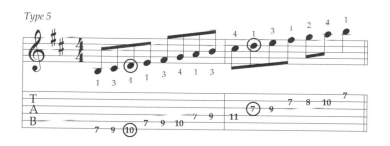

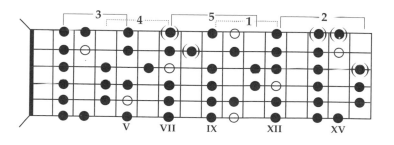

D Natural Minor (Aeolian)

WHWWHWW

Type 1

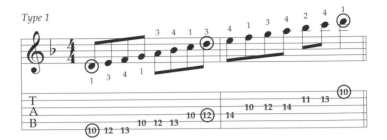

Type 2

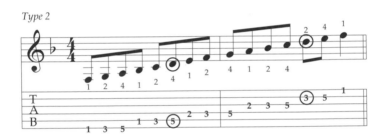

Type 3

58

Type 4

Type 5

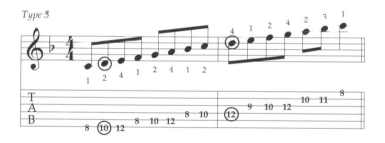

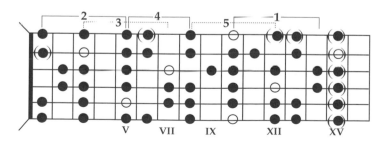

D Dorian

WHWWWHW

Type 1

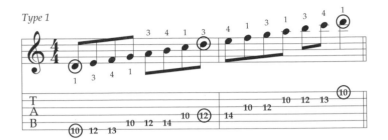

Type 2

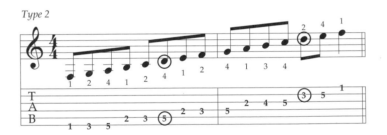

Type 3

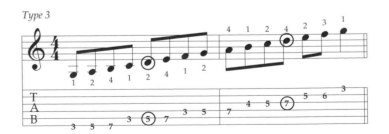

Type 4

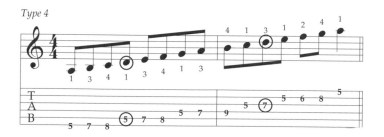

Type 5

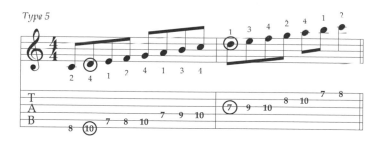

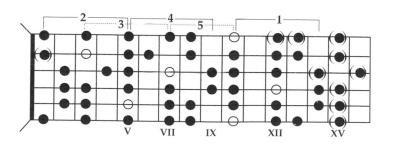

D Phrygian

HWWWHWW

Type 1

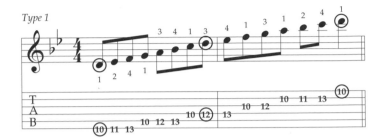

Type 2

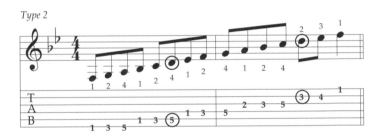

Type 3

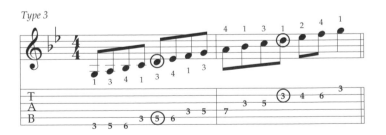

62

Type 4

Type 5

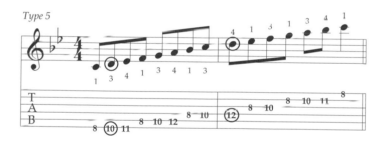

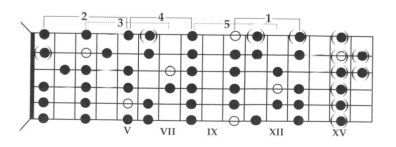

63

D Lydian

WWWHWWH

Type 1

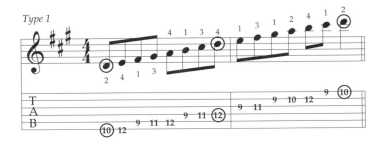

Type 2

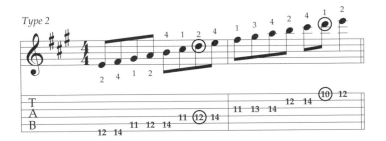

Type 3

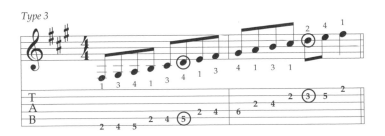

Type 4

Type 5

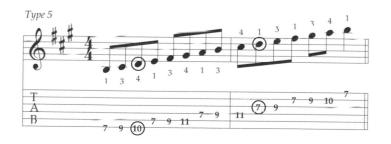

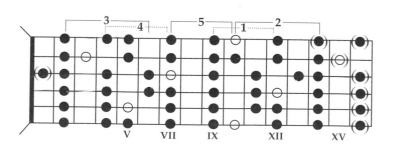

D Mixolydian

WWHWWHW

Type 1

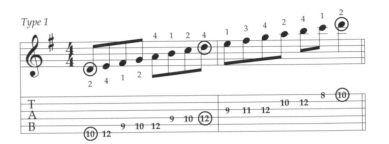

Type 2

Type 3

66

Type 4

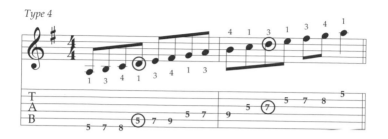

Type 5

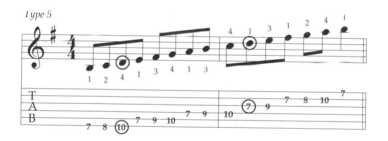

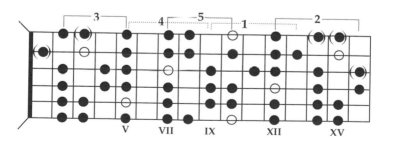

67

D Locrian

HWWHWWW

Type 1

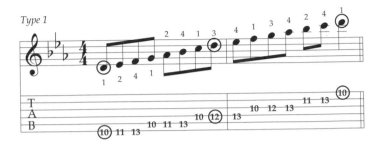

Type 2

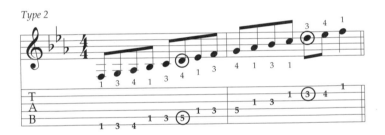

Type 3

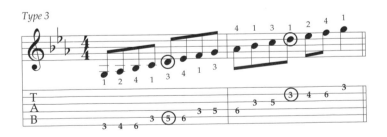

68

Type 4

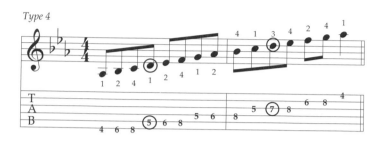

Type 5

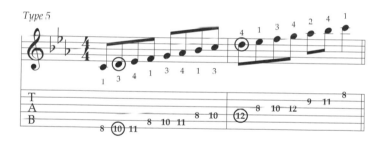

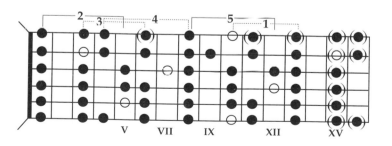

69

D Harmonic Minor

WHWWHm3H

Type 1

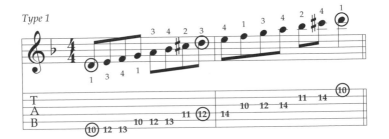

Type 2

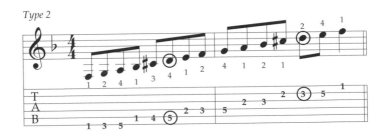

Type 3

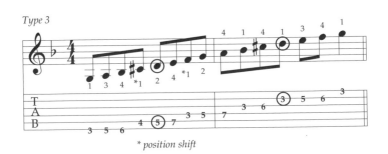

* position shift

70

Type 4

Type 5

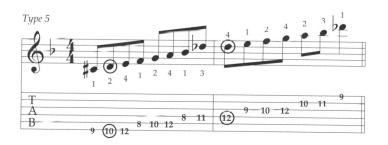

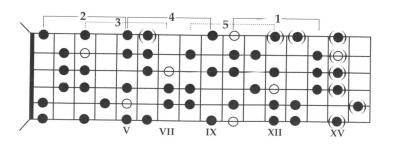

71

D Whole Tone

wwwwww

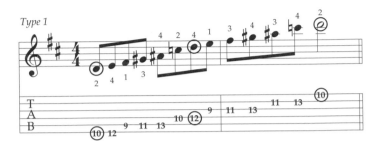

Type 1

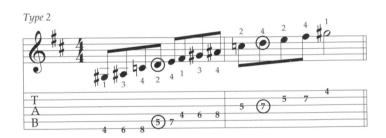

Type 2

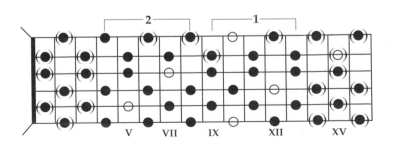

D Diminished (whole-half)

WHWHWHWH

Type 1

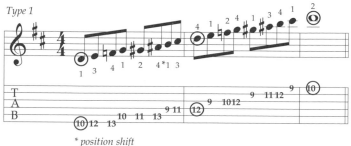

* position shift

Type 2

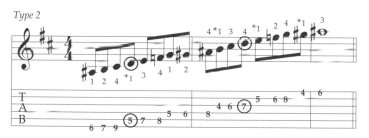

* position shift

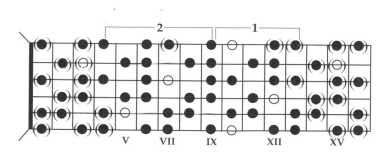

73

D Pentatonic (Major)

WWm3Wm3

Type 1

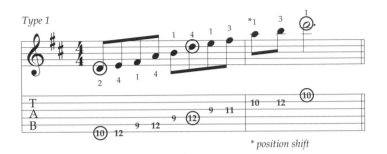

* position shift

Type 2

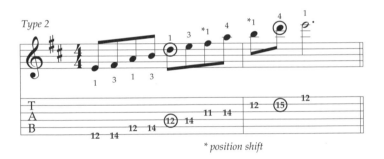

* position shift

Type 3

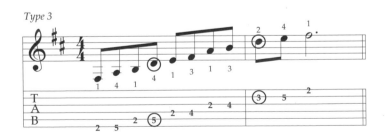

Type 4

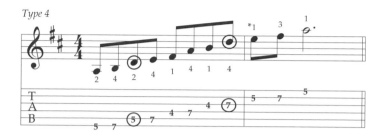

Type 5

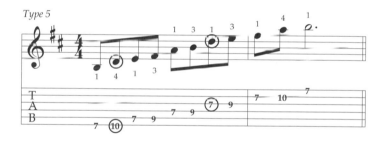

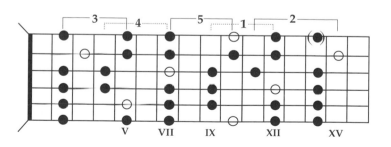

D Pentatonic (Minor)

m3WWm3W

Type 1

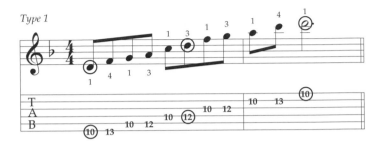

Type 2

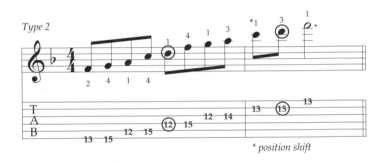

* *position shift*

Type 3

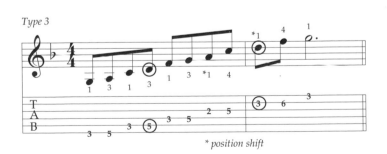

* *position shift*

Type 4

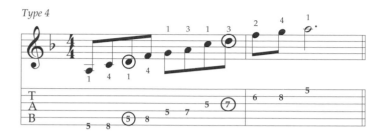

Type 5

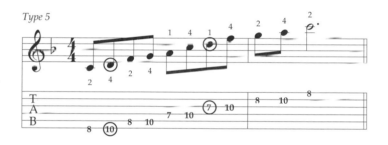

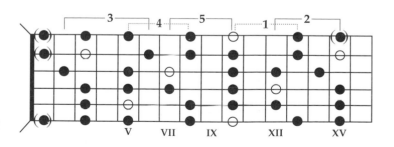

77

D Blues Scale
(with major 3rd & flattened 5th)

m3HHHHm3W

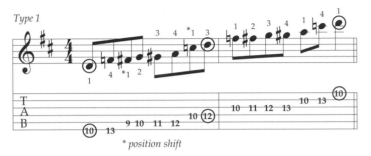

Type 1

* position shift

Type 2

* position shift

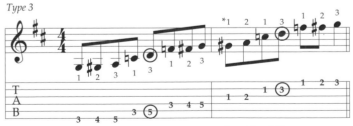

Type 3

* position shift

Type 4

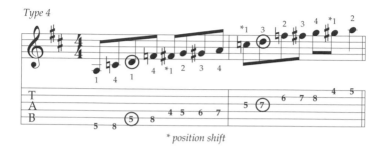

* position shift

Type 5

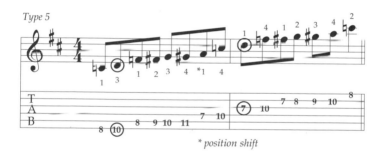

* position shift

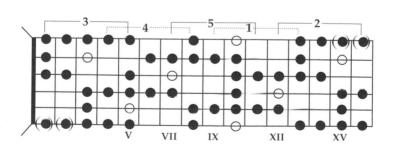

E♭ Major (Ionian)

WWHWWWH

Type 1

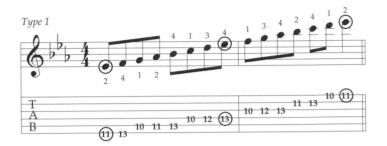

Type 2

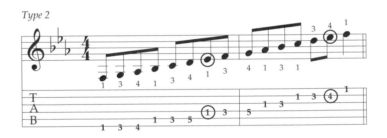

Type 3

Type 4

* position shift

Type 5

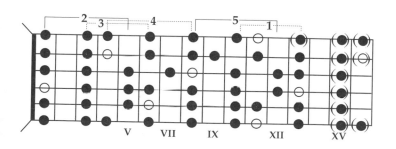

E♭ Natural Minor (Aeolian)

WHWWHWW

Type 1

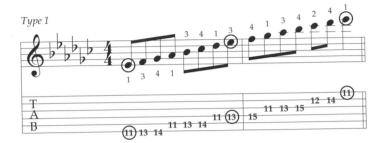

Type 2

Type 3

Type 4

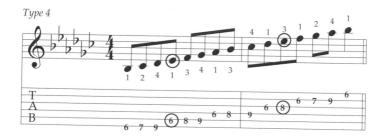

Type 5

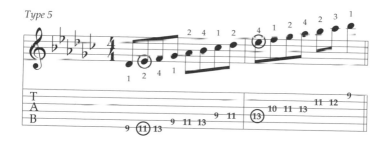

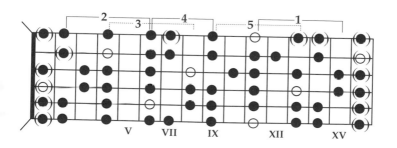

83

E♭ Dorian

WHWWWHW

Type 1

Type 2

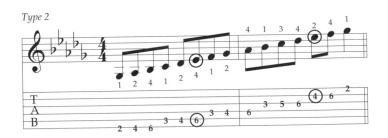

Type 3

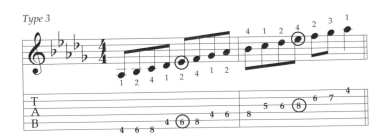

Type 4

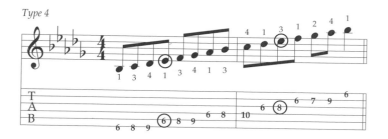

Type 5

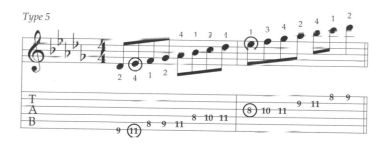

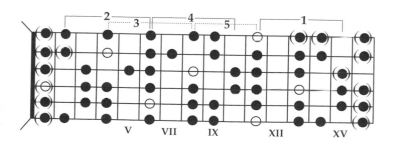

85

E♭ Phrygian

HWWWHWW

Type 1

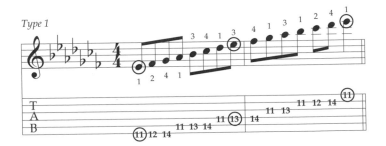

Type 2

Type 3

86

Type 4

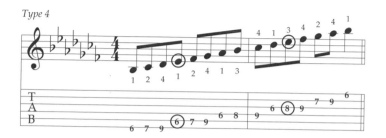

Type 5

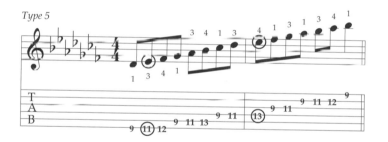

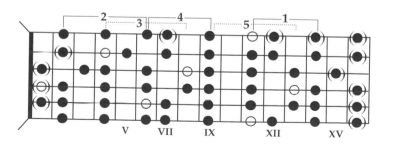

87

E♭ Lydian

WWWHWWH

Type 1

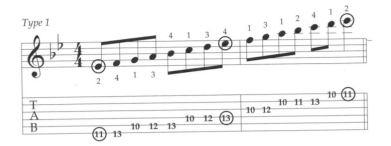

Type 2

Type 3

Type 4

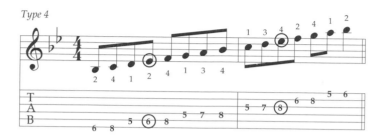

Type 5

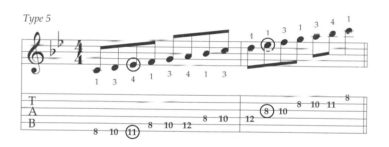

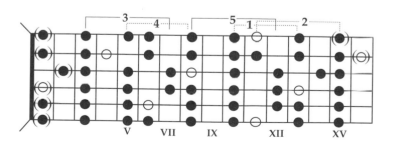

89

E♭ Mixolydian

WWHWWHW

Type 1

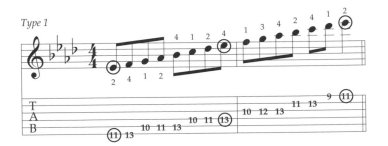

Type 2

Type 3

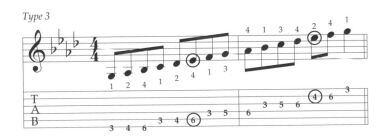

90

Type 4

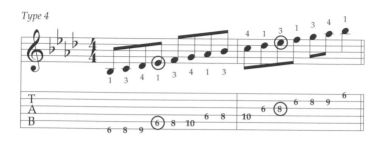

Type 5

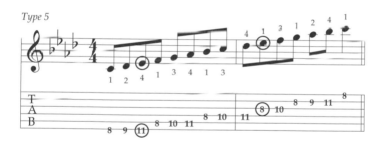

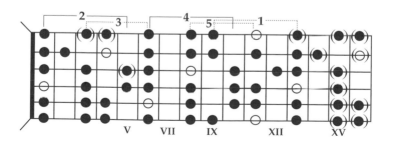

E♭ Locrian

HWWHWWW

Type 1

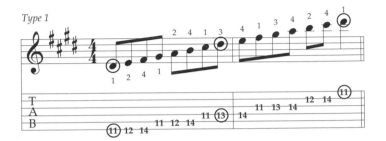

Type 2

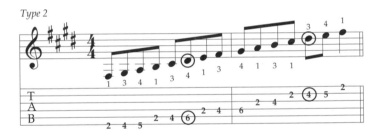

Type 3

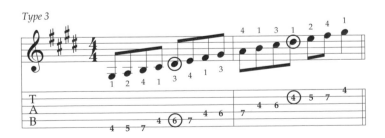

Type 4

Type 5

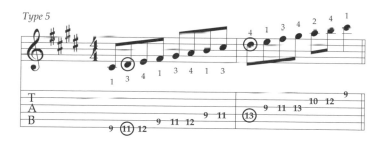

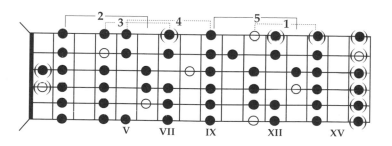

93

E♭ Harmonic Minor

WHWWHm3H

Type 1

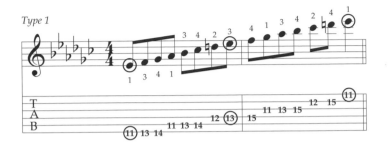

Type 2

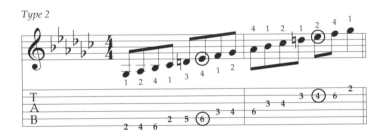

Type 3

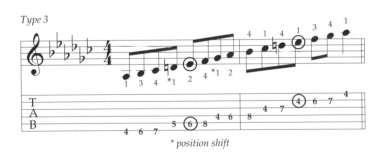

* position shift

94

Type 4

Type 5

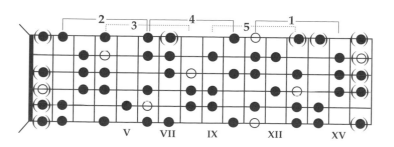

95

E♭ Whole Tone

wwwwww

Type 1

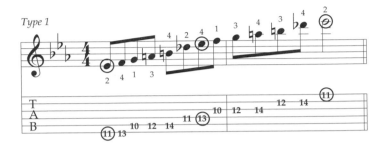

Type 2

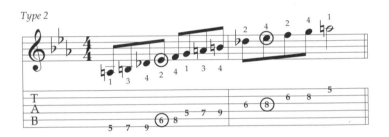

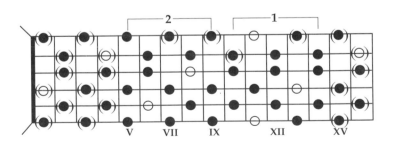

E♭ Diminished (whole-half)

WHWHWHWH

Type 1

* position shift

Type 2

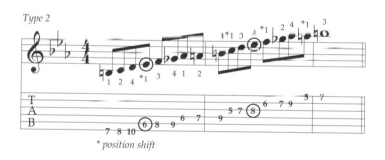

* position shift

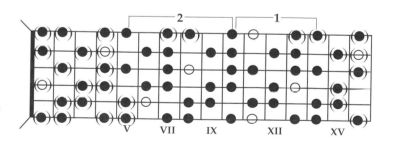

97

E♭ Pentatonic (Major)

WWm3Wm3

Type 1

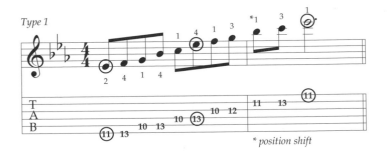

* position shift

Type 2

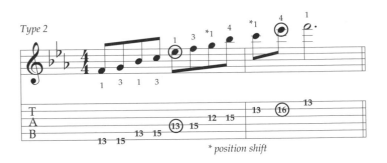

* position shift

Type 3

Type 4

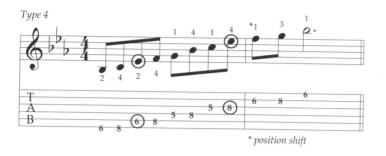

* position shift

Type 5

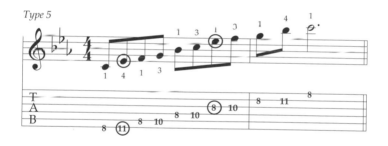

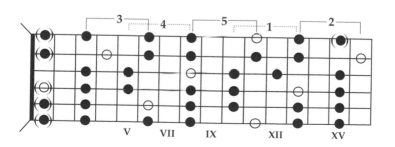

99

E♭ **Pentatonic (Minor)**

m3WWm3W

Type 1

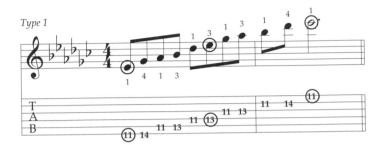

Type 2

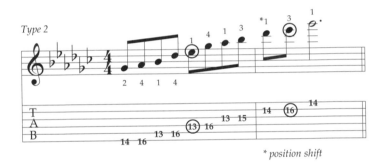

* position shift

Type 3

* position shift

Type 4

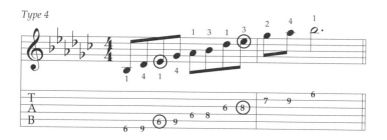

Type 5

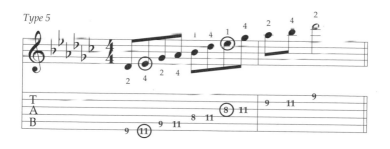

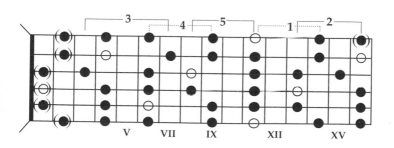

E♭ Blues Scale
(with major 3rd & flattened 5th)

m3HHHHm3W

Type 1

* position shift

Type 2

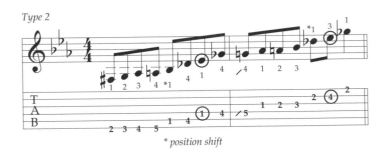

* position shift

Type 3

* position shift

Type 4

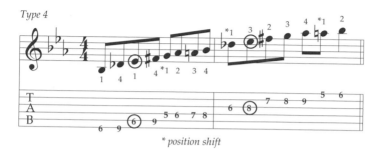

position shift

Type 5

position shift

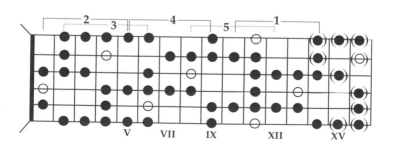

103

E Major (Ionian)

WWHWWWH

Type 1

Type 2

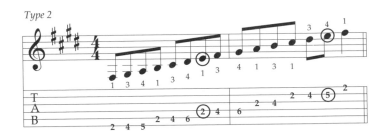

Type 3

Type 4

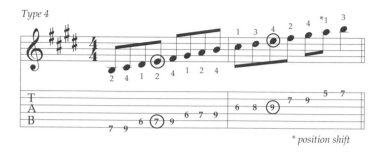

* position shift

Type 5

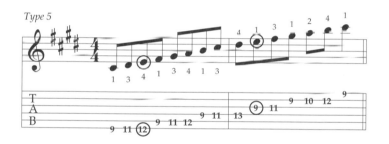

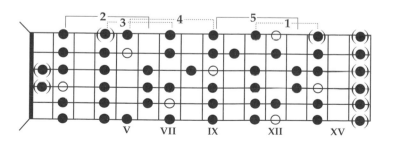

E Natural Minor (Aeolian)

WHWWHWW

Type 1

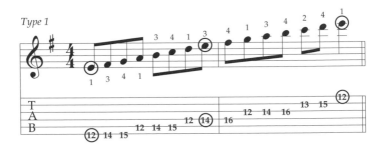

Type 2

Type 3

106

Type 4

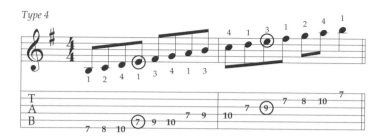

Type 5

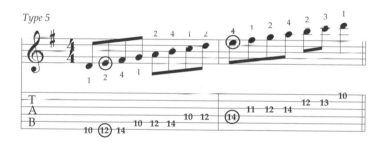

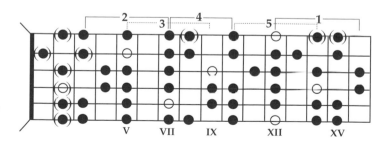

107

E Dorian

WHWWWHW

Type 1

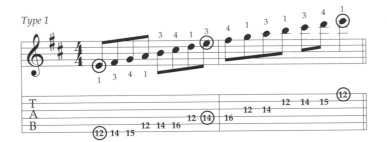

Type 2

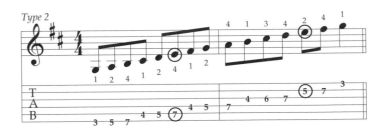

Type 3

108

Type 4

Type 5

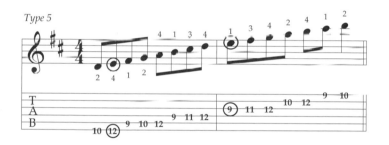

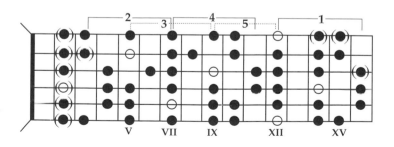

109

E Phrygian

HWWWHWW

Type 1

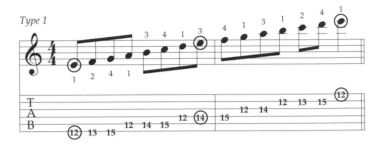

Type 2

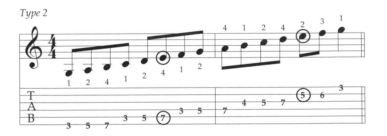

Type 3

Type 4

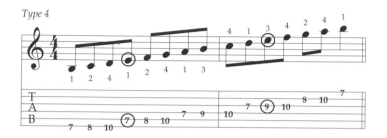

Type 5

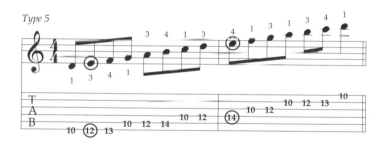

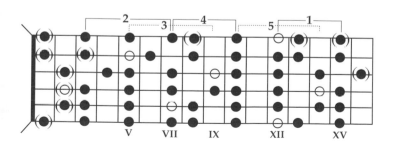

111

E Lydian

WWWHWWH

Type 1

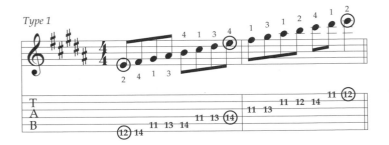

Type 2

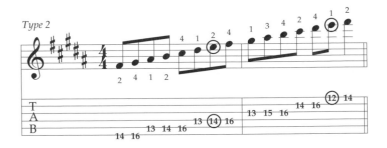

Type 3

112

Type 4

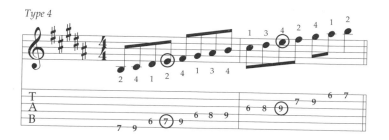

Type 5

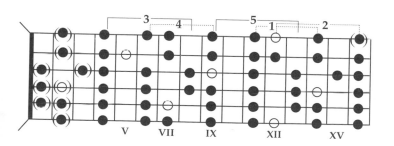

113

E Mixolydian

WWHWWHW

Type 1

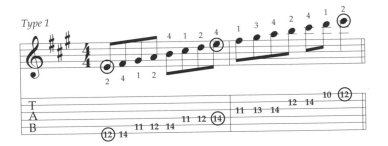

Type 2

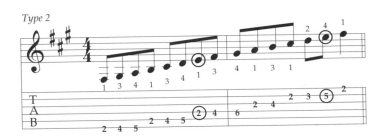

Type 3

Type 4

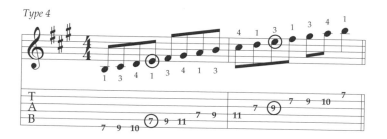

Type 5

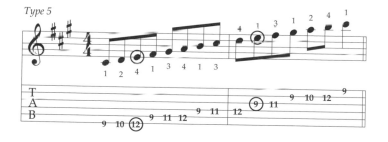

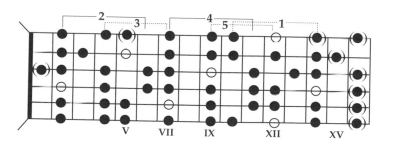

E Locrian

HWWHWWW

Type 1

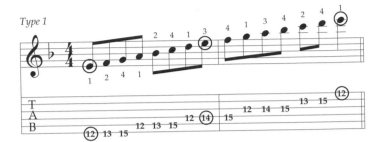

Type 2

Type 3

116

Type 4

Type 5

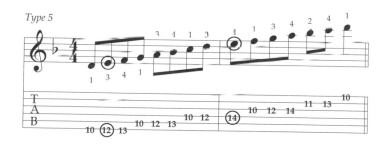

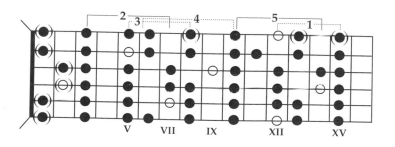

117

E Harmonic Minor

WHWWHm3H

Type 1

Type 2

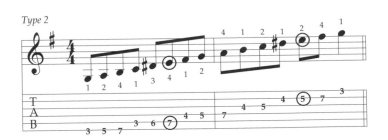

Type 3

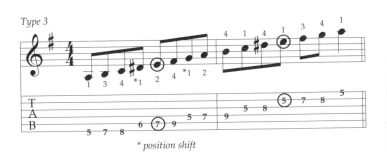

*position shift

118

Type 4

Type 5

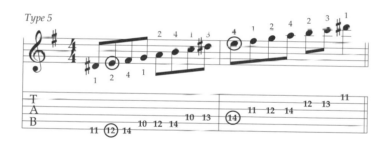

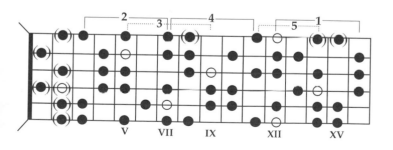

119

E Whole Tone

wwwwww

Type 1

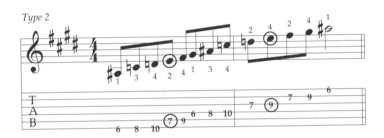

Type 2

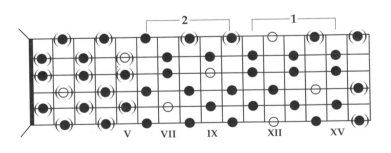

E Diminished (whole-half)

WHWHWHWH

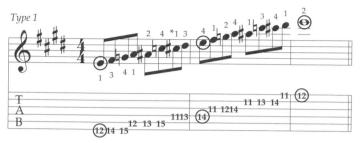

Type 1

* position shift

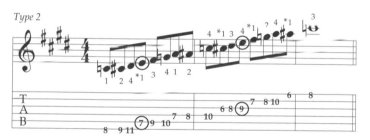

Type 2

* position shift

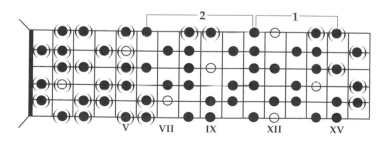

121

E Pentatonic (Major)

WWm3Wm3

Type 1

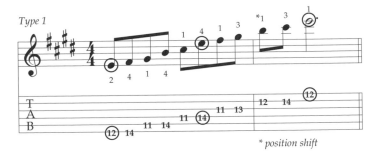

* position shift

Type 2

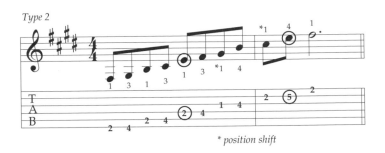

* position shift

Type 3

Type 4

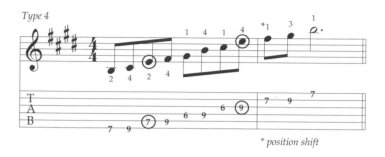

* position shift

Type 5

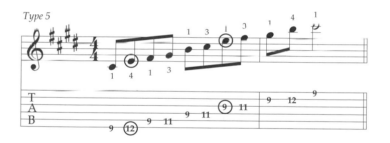

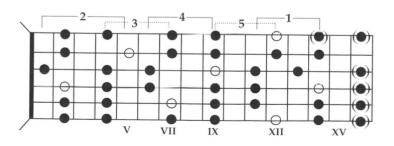

123

E Pentatonic (Minor)

m3WWm3W

Type 1

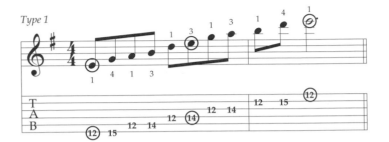

Type 2

* position shift

Type 3

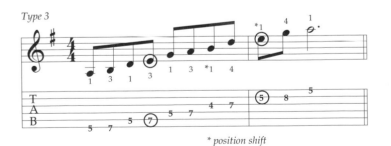

* position shift

124

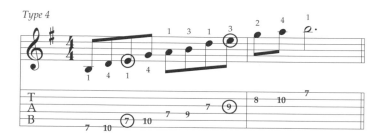

Type 4

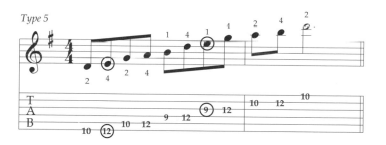

Type 5

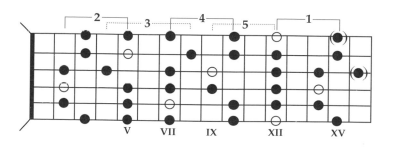

E Blues Scale
(with major 3rd & flattened 5th)

m3HHHHm3W

Type 1

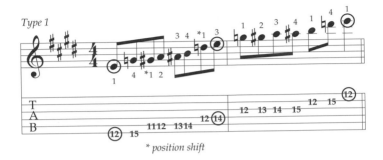

* position shift

Type 2

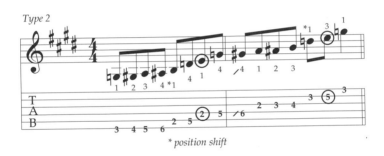

* position shift

Type 3

* position shift

Type 4

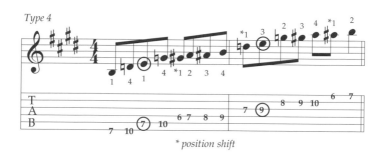

*position shift

Type 5

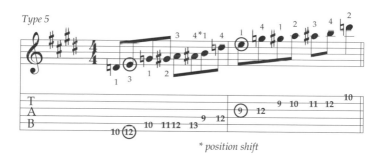

*position shift

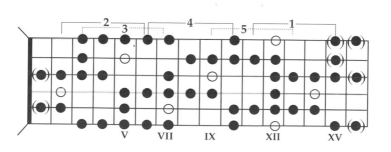

127

F Major (Ionian)

WWHWWWH

Type 1

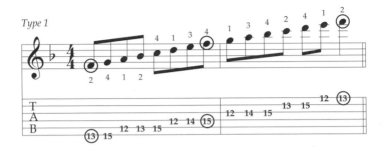

Type 2

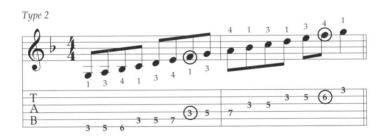

Type 3

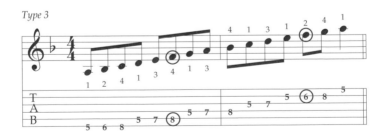

128

Type 4

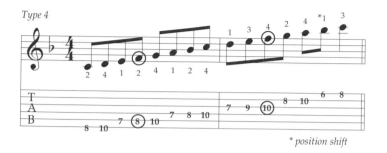

* position shift

Type 5

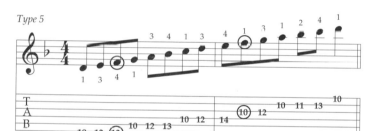

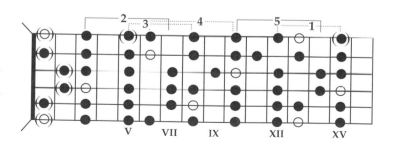

F Natural Minor (Aeolian)

WHWWHWW

Type 1

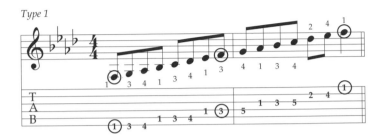

Type 2

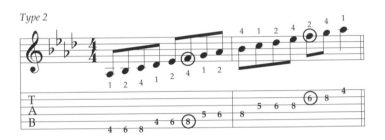

Type 3

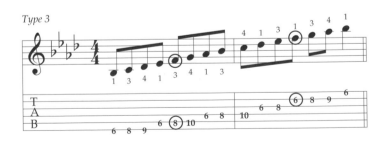

130

Type 4

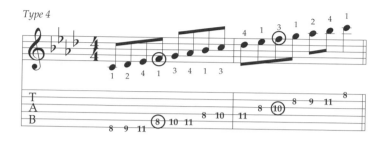

Type 5

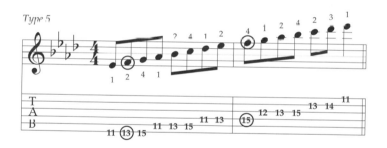

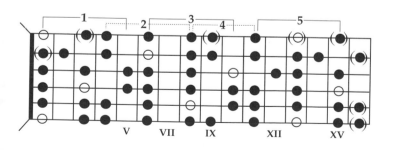

131

F Dorian

WHWWWHW

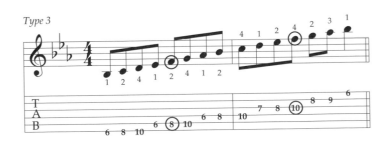

Type 4

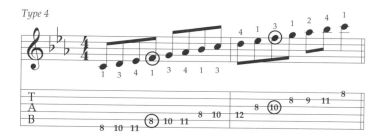

Type 5

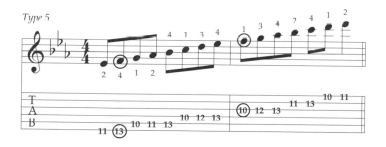

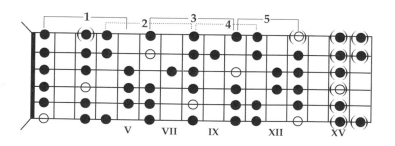

133

F Phrygian

HWWWHWW

Type 1

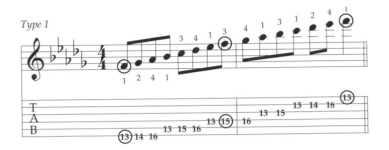

Type 2

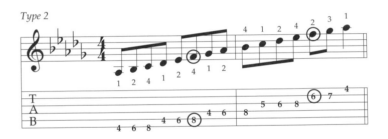

Type 3

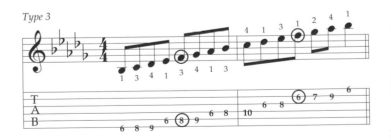

Type 4

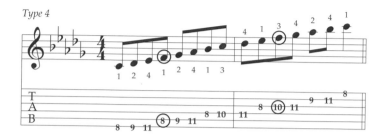

Type 5

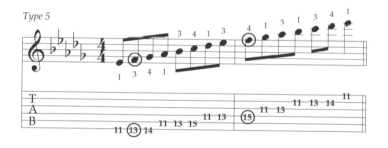

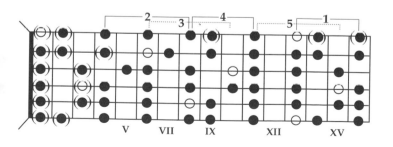

F Lydian

WWWHWWH

Type 1

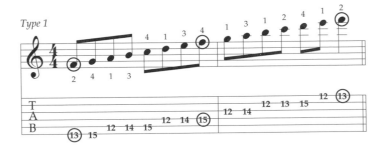

Type 2

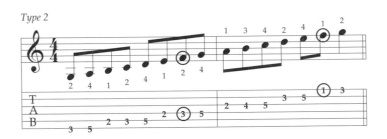

Type 3

136

Type 4

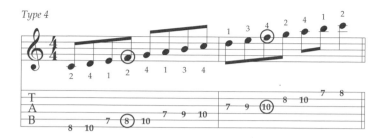

Type 5

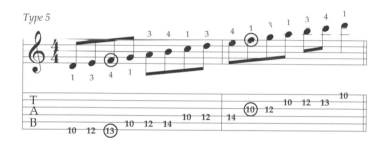

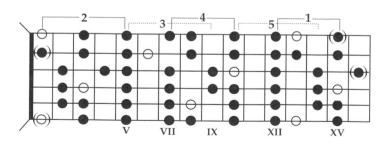

137

F Mixolydian

WWHWWHW

Type 1

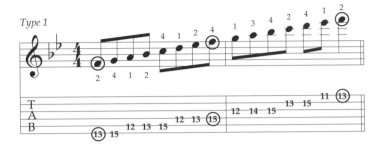

Type 2

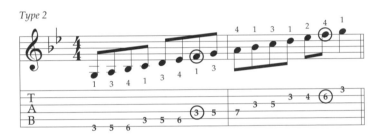

Type 3

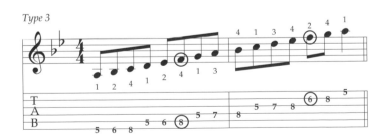

138

Type 4

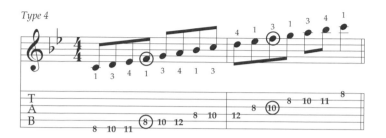

Type 5

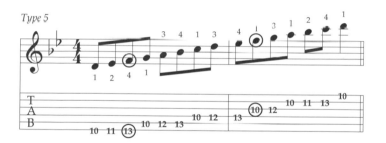

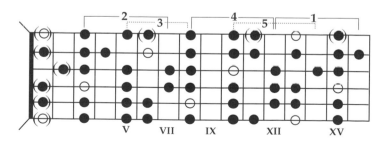

F Locrian

HWWHWWW

Type 1

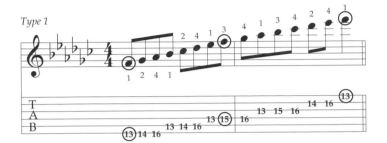

Type 2

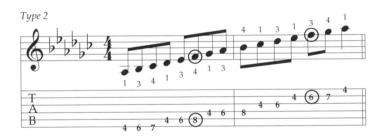

Type 3

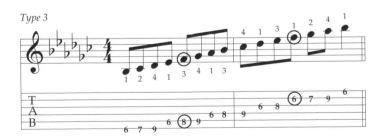

140

Type 4

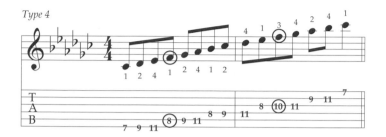

Type 5

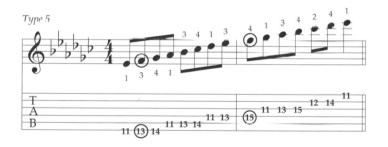

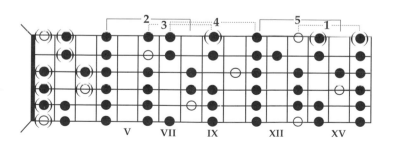

141

F Harmonic Minor

WHWWHm3H

Type 1

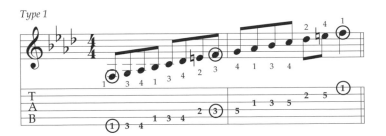

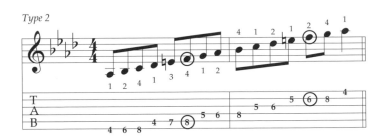

Type 2

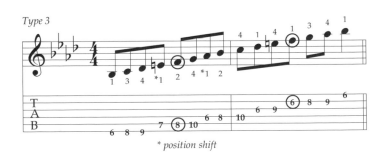

Type 3

* position shift

142

Type 4

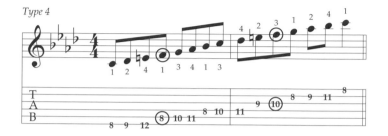

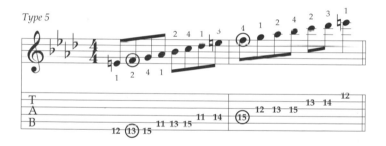

Type 5

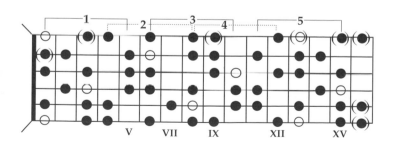

143

F Whole Tone

WWWWWW

Type 1

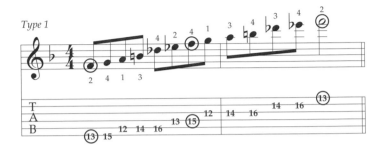

Type 2

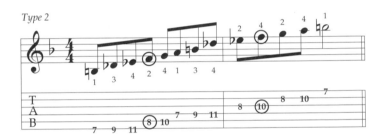

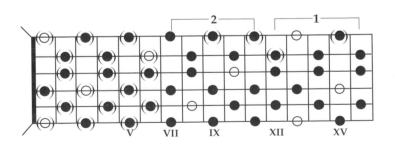

F Diminished (whole-half)

WHWHWHWH

Type 1

* position shift

Type 2

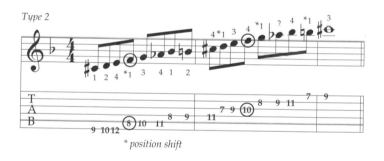

* position shift

145

F Pentatonic (Major)

WWm3Wm3

Type 1

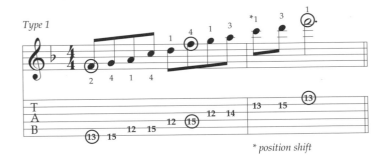

* position shift

Type 2

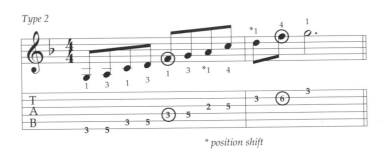

* position shift

Type 3

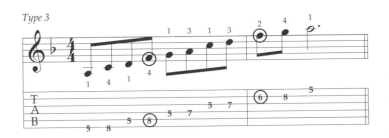

Type 4

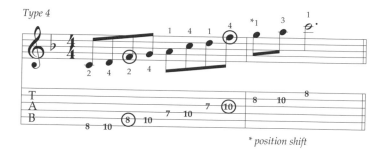

* position shift

Type 5

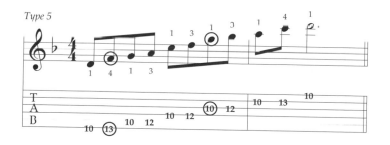

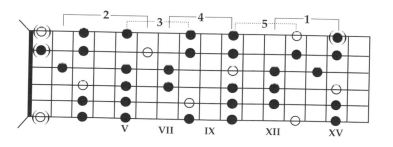

F Pentatonic (Minor)

m3WWm3W

Type 1

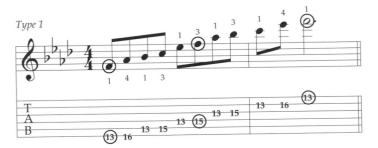

Type 2

* position shift

Type 3

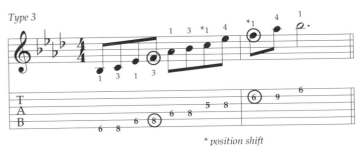

* position shift

148

Type 4

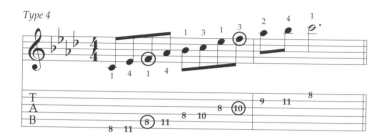

Type 5

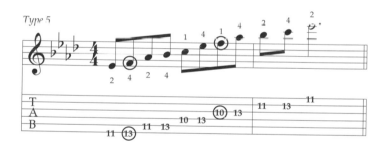

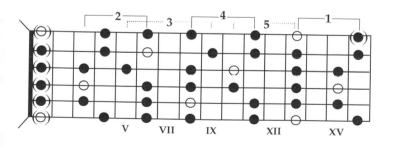

149

F Blues Scale
(with major 3rd & flattened 5th)

m3HHHHm3W

Type 1

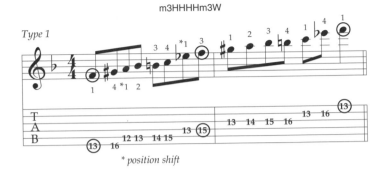

* position shift

Type 2

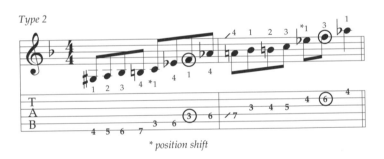

* position shift

Type 3

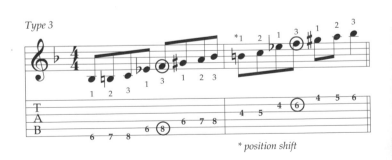

* position shift

150

Type 4

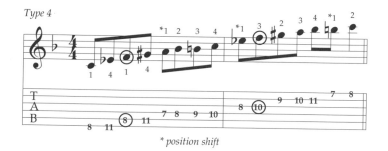

* position shift

Type 5

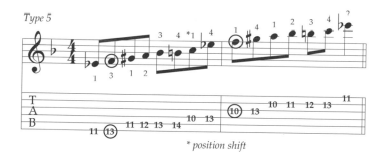

* position shift

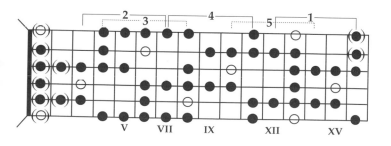

F♯ Major (Ionian)

WWHWWWH

Type 1

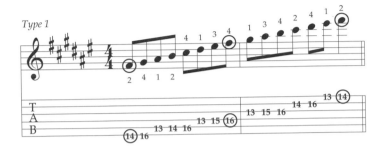

Type 2

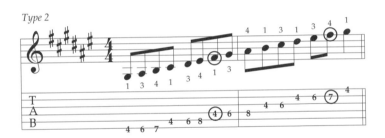

Type 3

Type 4

* position shift

Type 5

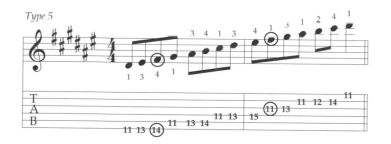

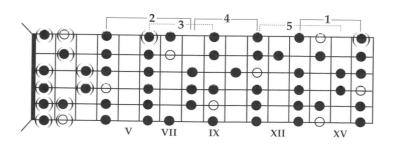

F♯ Natural Minor (Aeolian)

WHWWHWW

Type 1

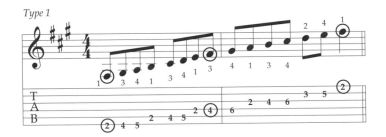

Type 2

Type 3

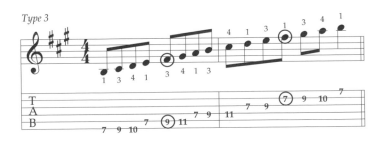

Type 4

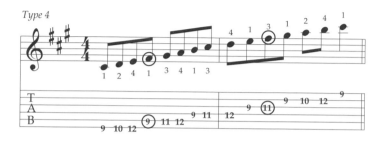

Type 5

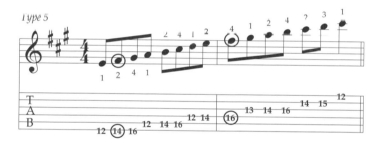

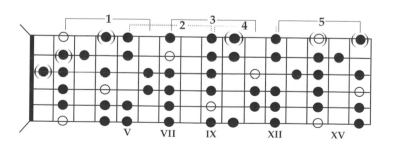

155

F# Dorian

WHWWWHW

Type 1

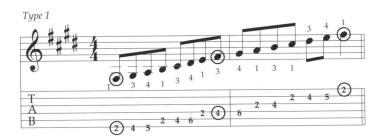

Type 2

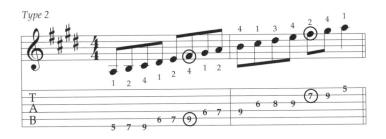

Type 3

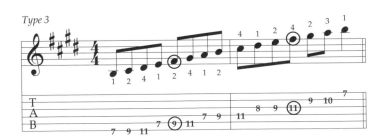

156

Type 4

Type 5

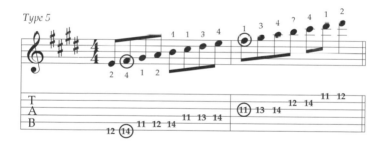

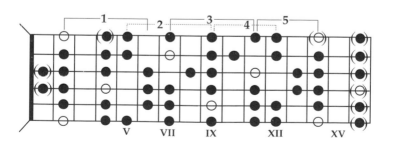

157

F# Phrygian

HWWWHWW

Type 1

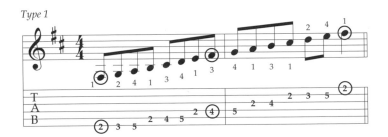

Type 2

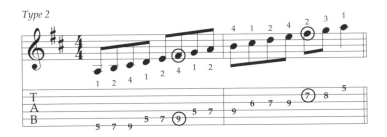

Type 3

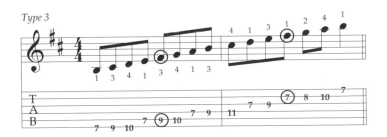

Type 4

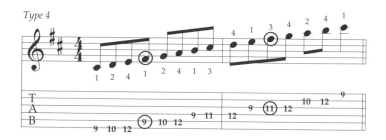

Type 5

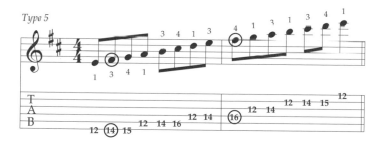

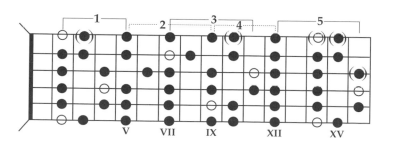

159

F# Lydian

WWWHWWH

Type 1

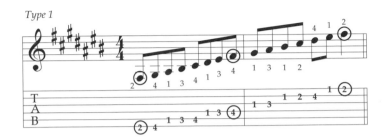

Type 2

Type 3

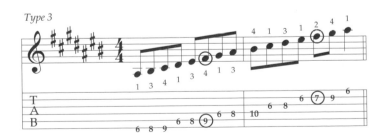

Type 4

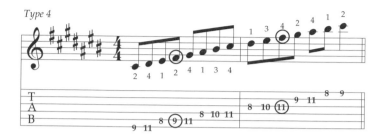

Type 5

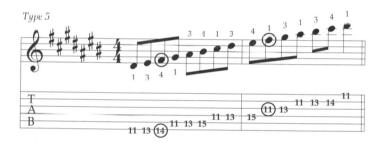

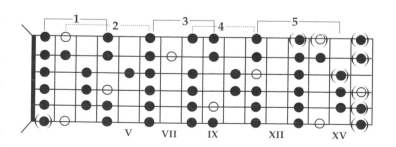

F# Mixolydian

WWHWWHW

Type 1

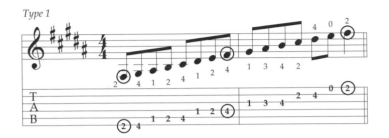

Type 2

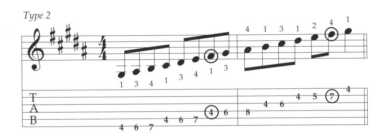

Type 3

162

Type 4

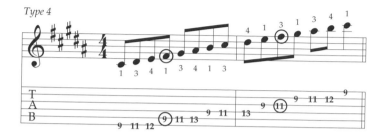

Type 5

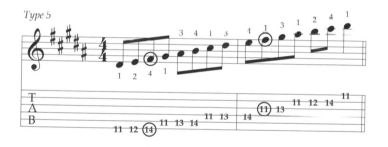

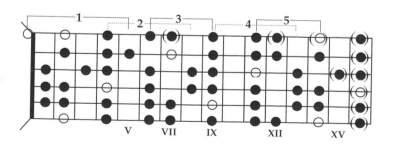

163

F# Locrian

HWWHWWW

Type 1

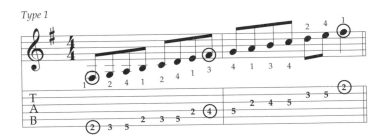

Type 2

Type 3

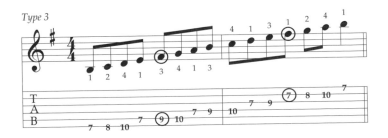

164

Type 4

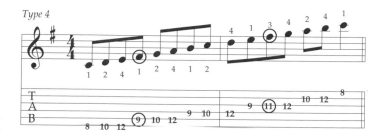

Type 5

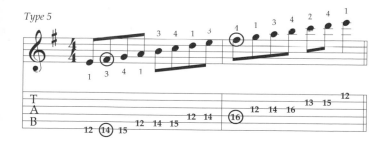

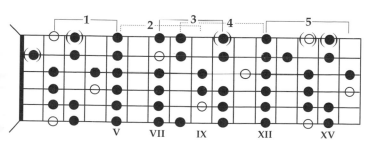

165

F♯ Harmonic Minor

WHWWHm3H

Type 1

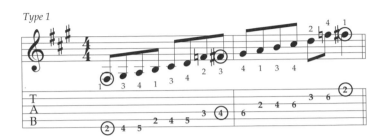

Type 2

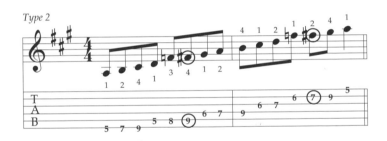

Type 3

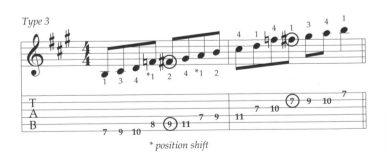

* position shift

166

Type 4

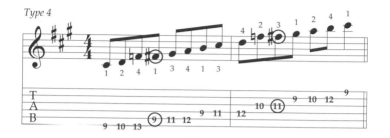

Type 5

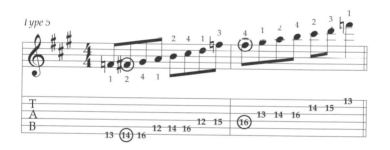

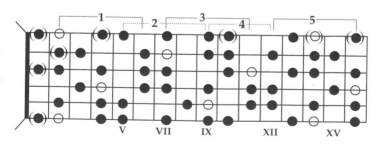

F# Whole Tone

wwwwww

Type 1

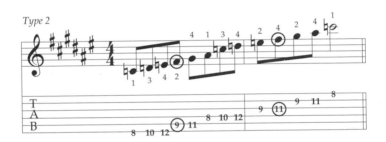

Type 2

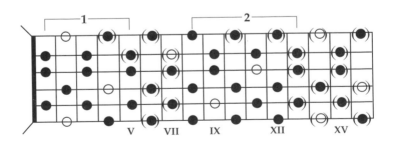

F# Diminished (whole-half)

WHWHWHWH

Type 1

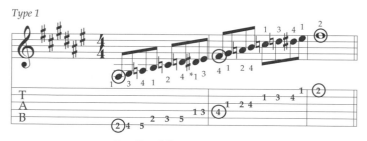

* *position shift*

Type 2

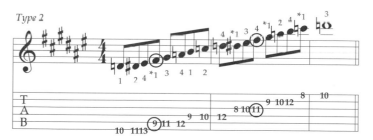

* *position shift*

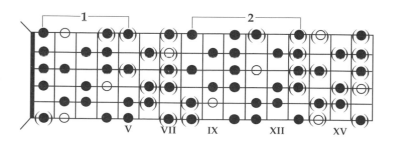

F♯ Pentatonic (Major)

WWm3Wm3

Type 1

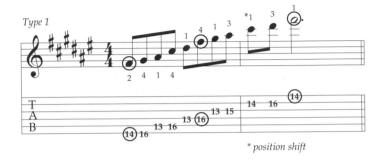

* position shift

Type 2

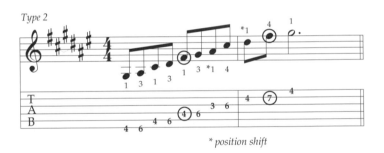

* position shift

Type 3

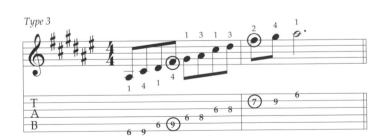

Type 4

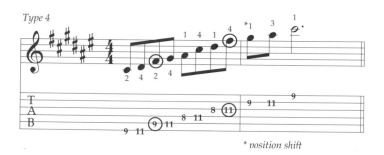

* position shift

Type 5

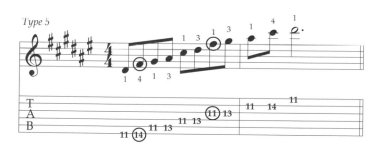

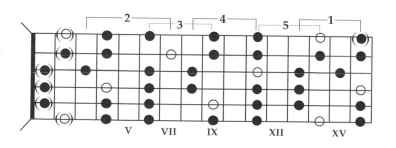

F♯ Pentatonic (Minor)

m3WWm3W

Type 1

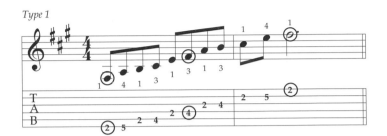

Type 2

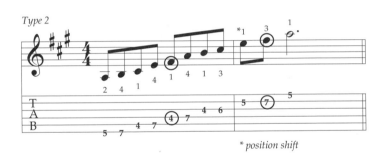

* position shift

Type 3

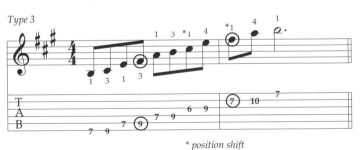

* position shift

Type 4

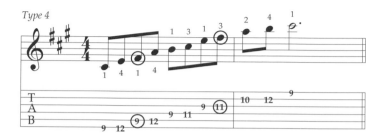

Type 5

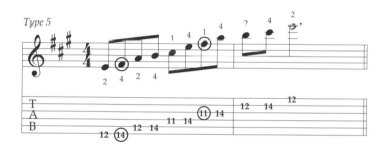

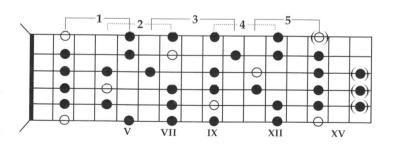

173

F# Blues Scale
(with major 3rd & flattened 5th)

m3HHHHm3W

Type 1

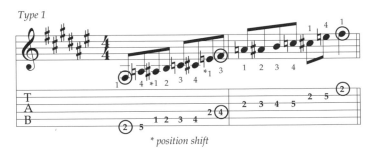

* position shift

Type 2

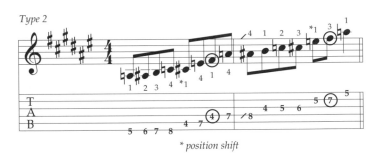

* position shift

Type 3

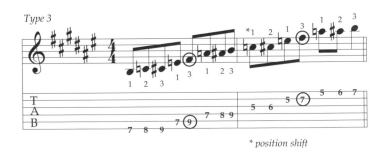

* position shift

174

Type 4

* position shift

Type 5

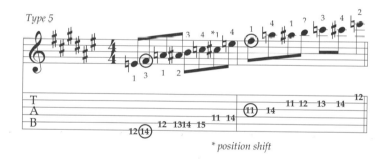

* position shift

175

G Major (Ionian)

WWHWWWH

Type 1

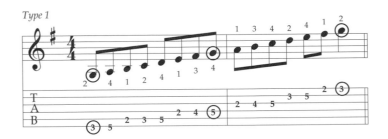

Type 2

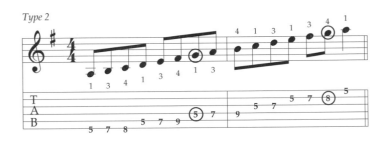

Type 3

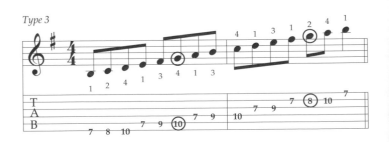

Type 4

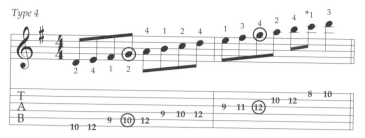

* position shift

Type 5

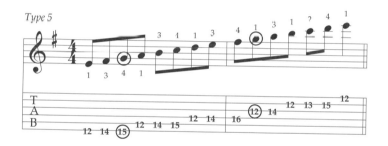

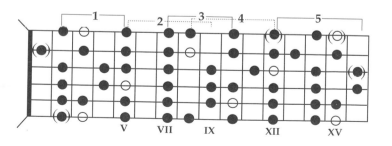

G Natural Minor (Aeolian)

WHWWHWW

Type 1

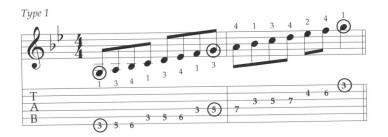

Type 2

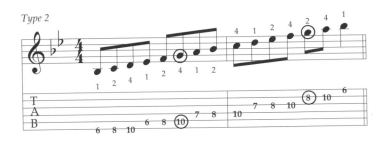

Type 3

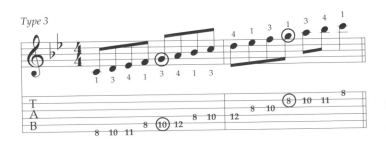

178

Type 4

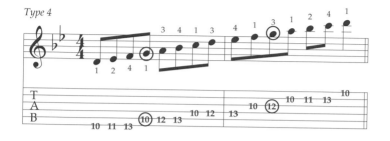

Type 5

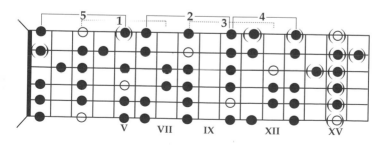

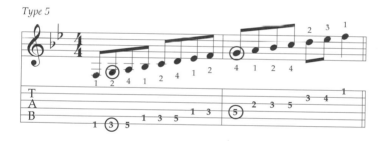

G Dorian

WHWWWHW

Type 1

Type 2

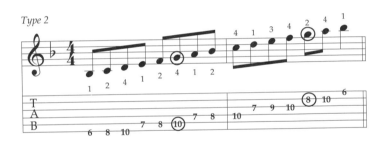

Type 3

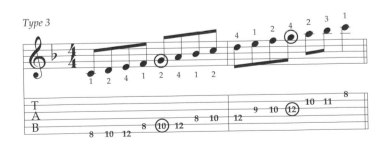

Type 4

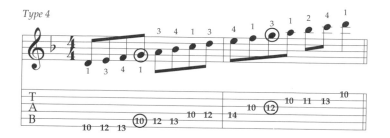

Type 5

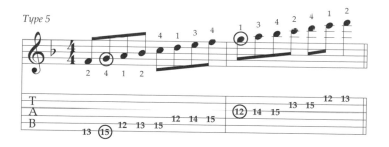

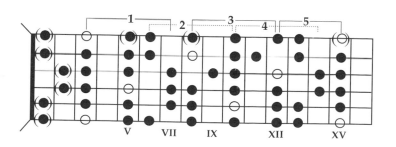

181

G Phrygian

HWWWHWW

Type 1

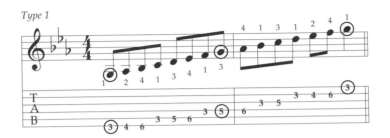

Type 2

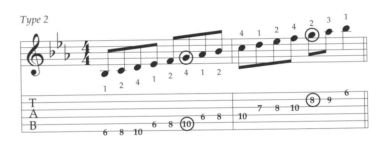

Type 3

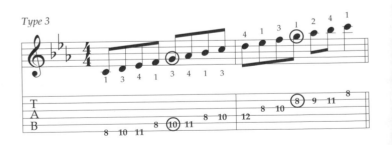

182

Type 4

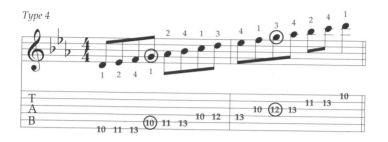

Type 5

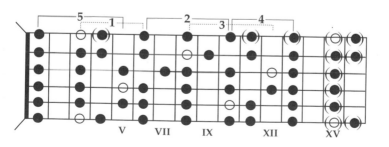

183

G Lydian

WWWHWWH

Type 1

Type 2

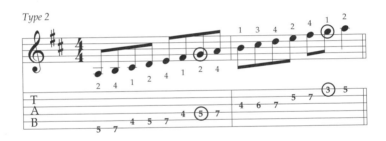

Type 3

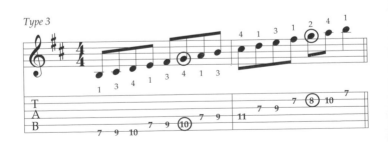

184

Type 4

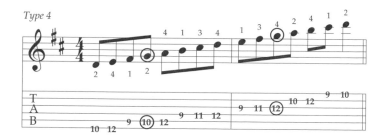

Type 5

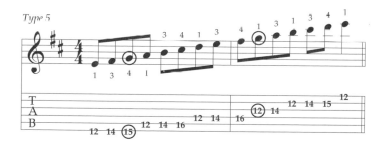

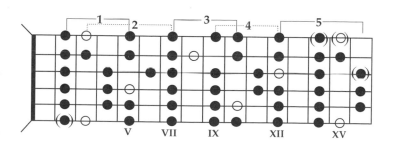

185

G Mixolydian

WWHWWHW

Type 1

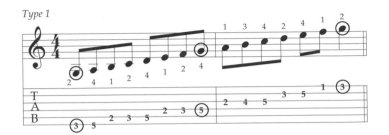

Type 2

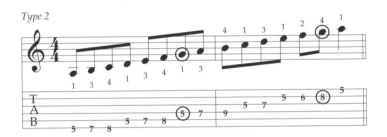

Type 3

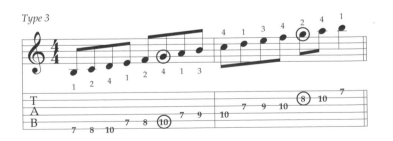

186

Type 4

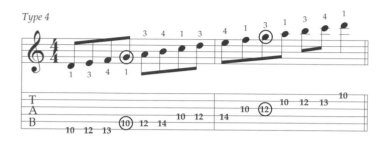

Type 5

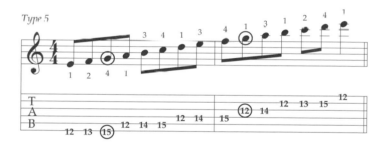

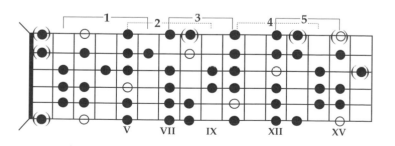

187

G Locrian

HWWHWWWH

Type 1

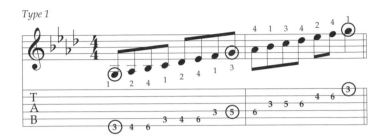

Type 2

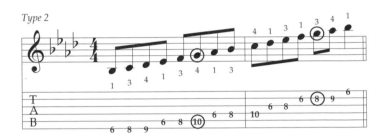

Type 3

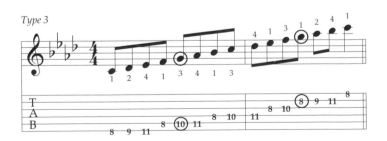

Type 4

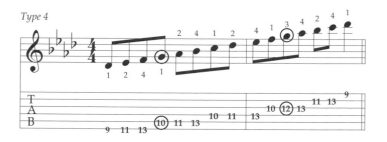

Type 5

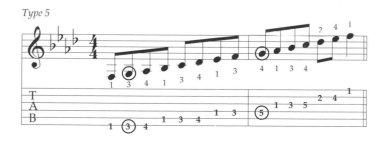

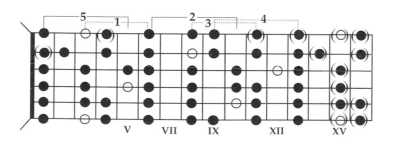

189

G Harmonic Minor

WHWWHm3H

Type 1

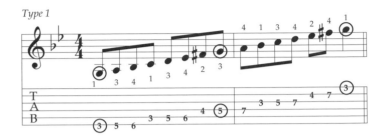

Type 2

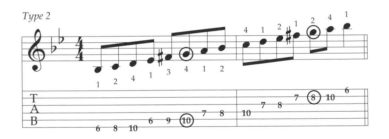

Type 3

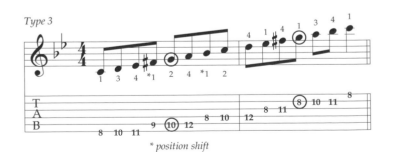

* position shift

190

Type 4

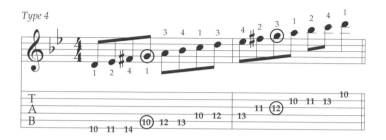

Type 5

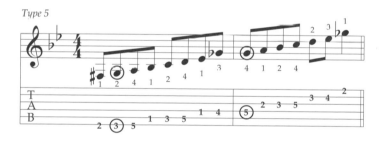

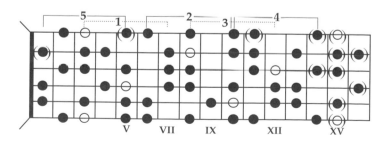

191

G Whole Tone

wwwwww

Type 1

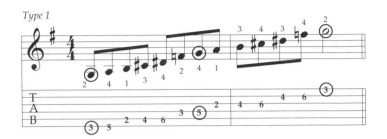

Type 2

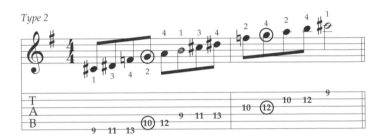

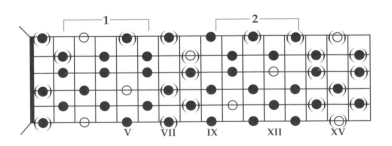

192

G Diminished (whole-half)

WHWHWHWH

Type 1

* position shift

Type 2

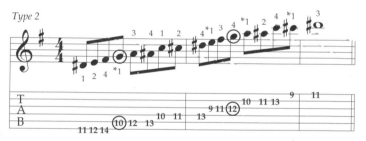

* position shift

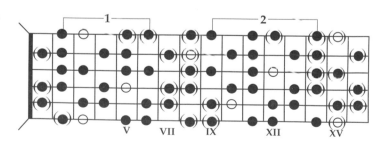

193

G Pentatonic (Major)

WWm3Wm3

Type 1

* position shift

Type 2

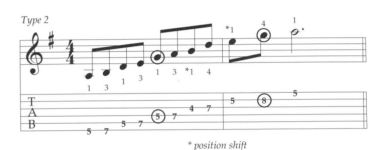

* position shift

Type 3

194

Type 4

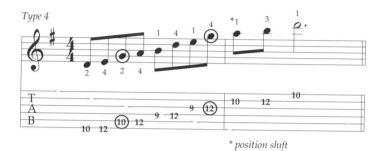

* position shift

Type 5

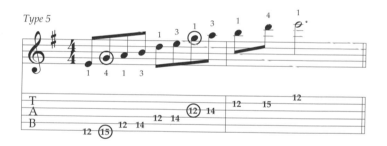

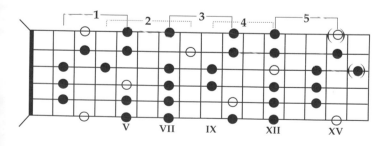

G Pentatonic (Minor)

m3WWm3W

Type 1

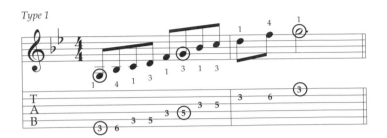

Type 2

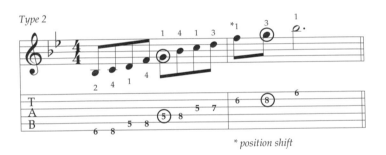

* position shift

Type 3

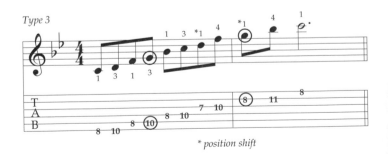

* position shift

196

Type 4

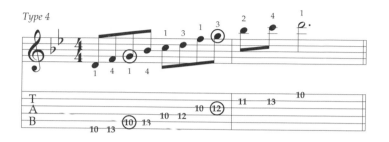

Type 5

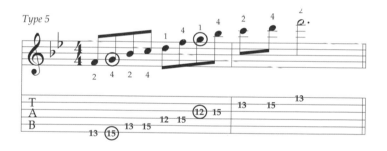

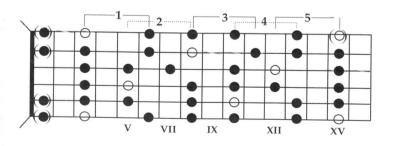

197

G Blues Scale
(with major 3rd & flattened 5th)

m3HHHHm3W

Type 1

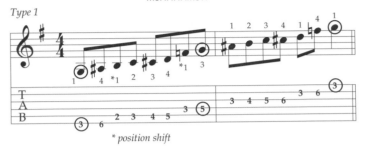

* position shift

Type 2

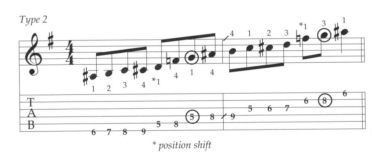

* position shift

Type 3

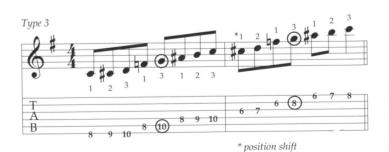

* position shift

198

Type 4

* position shift

Type 5

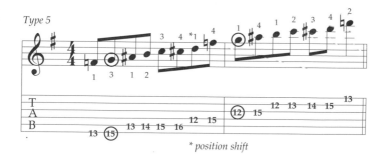

* position shift

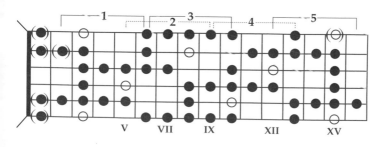

199

A♭ Major (Ionian)

WWHWWWH

Type 1

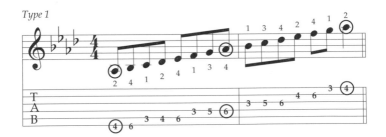

Type 2

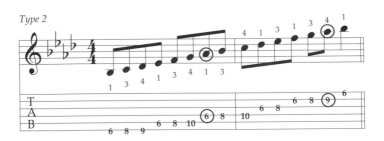

Type 3

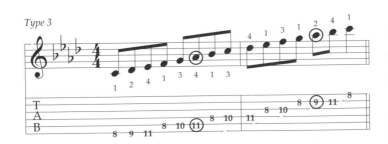

200

Type 4

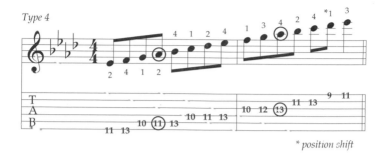

* position shift

Type 5

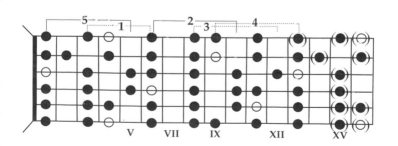

A♭ Natural Minor (Aeolian)

WHWWHWW

Type 1

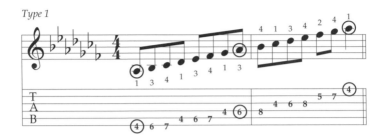

Type 2

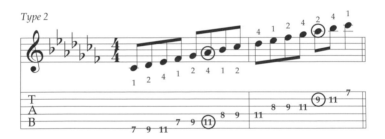

Type 3

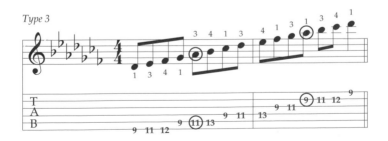

Type 4

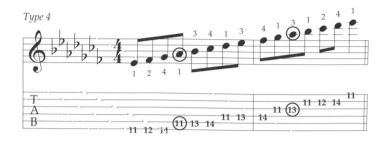

Type 5

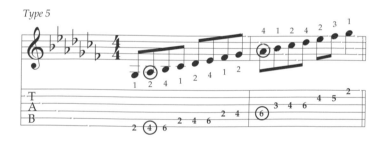

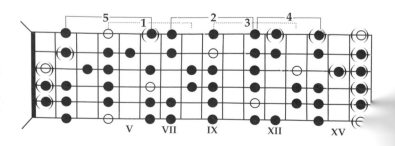

A♭ Dorian

WHWWWHW

Type 1

Type 2

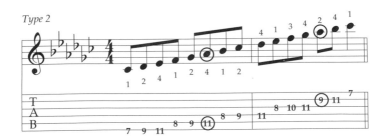

Type 3

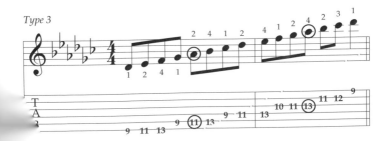

204

Type 4

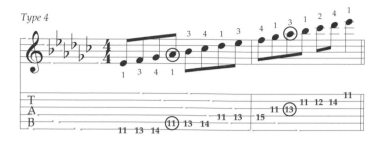

Type 5

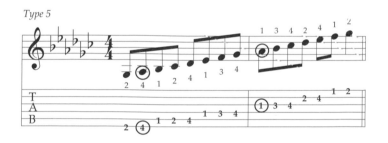

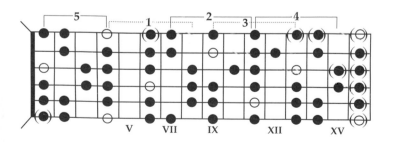

205

A♭ Phrygian

HWWWHWW

Type 1

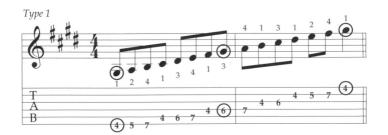

Type 2

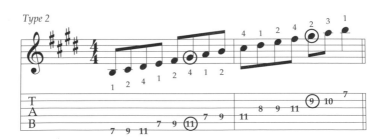

Type 3

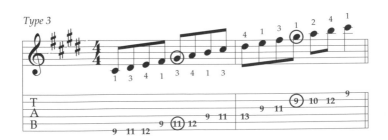

Type 4

Type 5

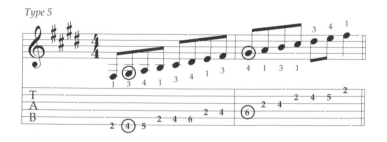

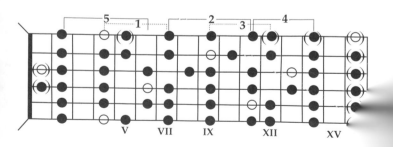

207

A♭ Lydian

WWWHWWH

Type 1

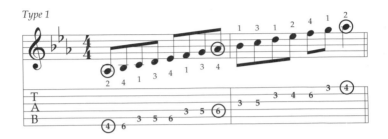

Type 2

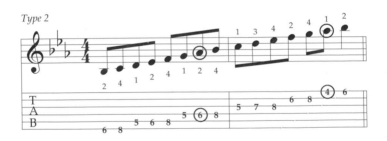

Type 3

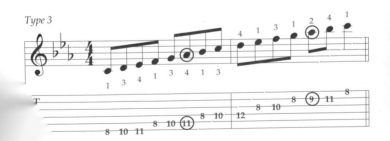

208

Type 4

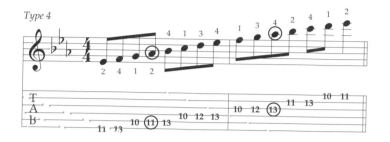

Type 5

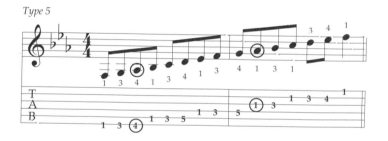

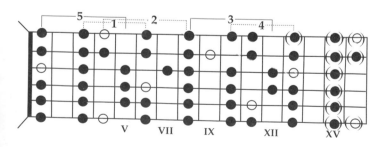

A♭ Mixolydian

WWHWWHW

Type 1

Type 2

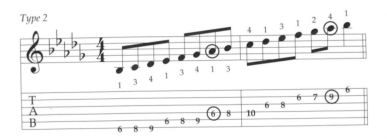

Type 3

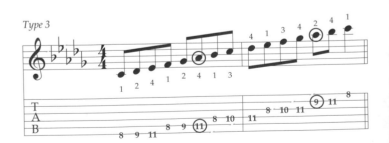

Type 4

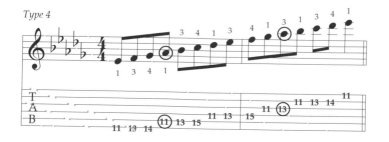

Type 5

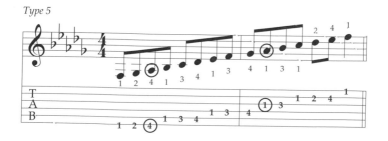

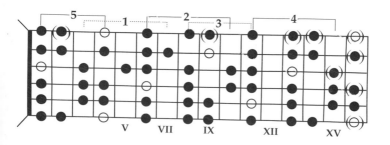

211

A♭ Locrian

HWWHWWW

Type 1

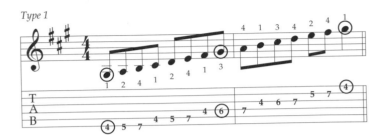

Type 2

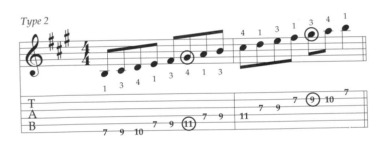

Type 3

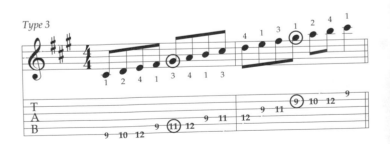

Type 4

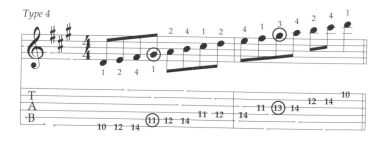

Type 5

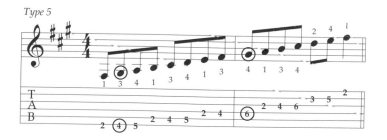

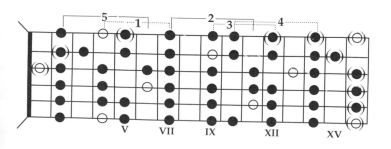

213

A♭ Harmonic Minor

WHWWHm3H

Type 1

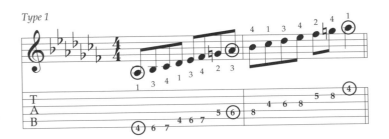

Type 2

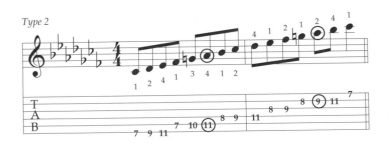

Type 3

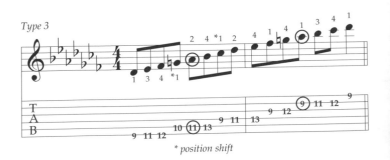

* position shift

214

Type 4

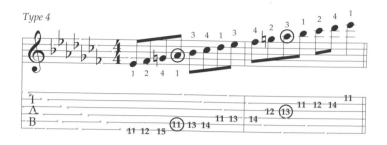

Type 5

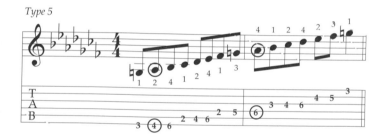

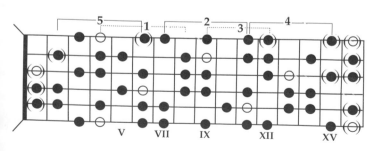

A♭ Whole Tone

wwwwww

Type 1

Type 2

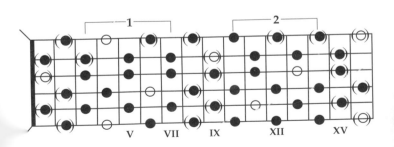

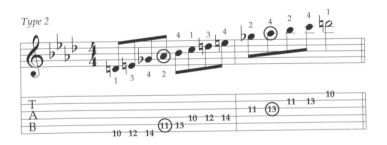

A♭ Diminished (whole-half)

WHWHWHWH

Type 1

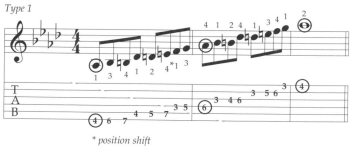

* position shift

Type 2

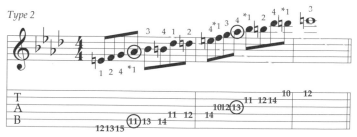

* position shift

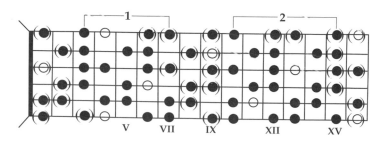

217

A♭ Pentatonic (Major)

WWm3Wm3

Type 1

* position shift

Type 2

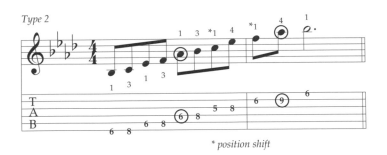

* position shift

Type 3

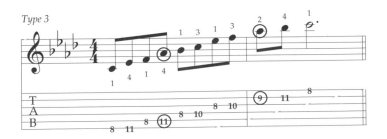

218

Type 4

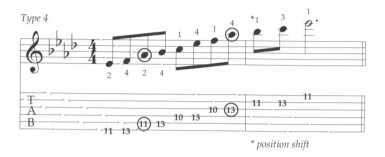

* position shift

Type 5

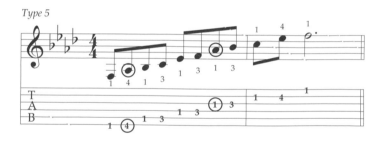

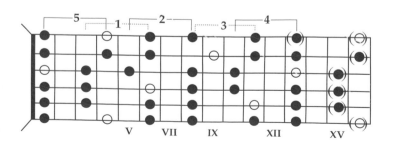

A♭ Pentatonic (Minor)

m3WWm3W

Type 1

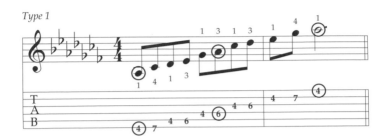

Type 2

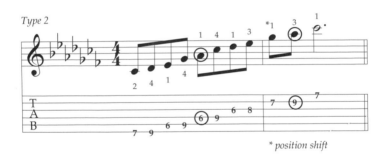

* position shift

Type 3

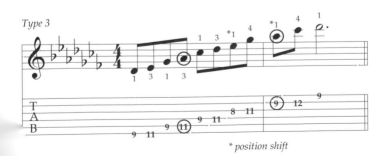

* position shift

Type 4

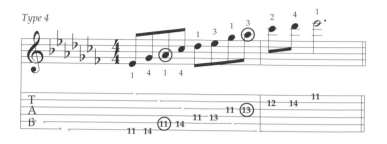

Type 5

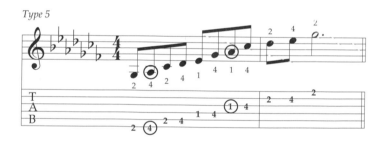

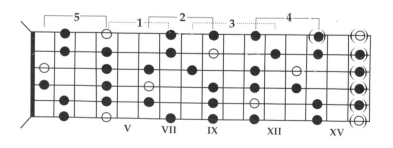

221

A♭ Blues Scale
(with major 3rd & flattened 5th)

m3HHHHm3W

Type 1

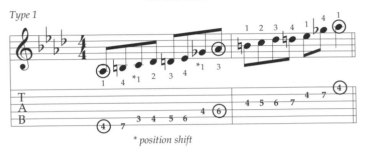

* position shift

Type 2

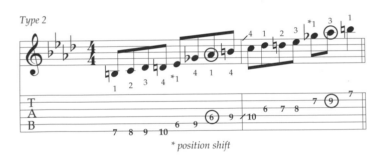

* position shift

Type 3

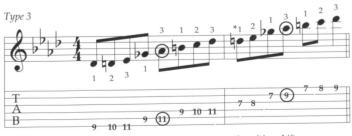

* position shift

Type 4

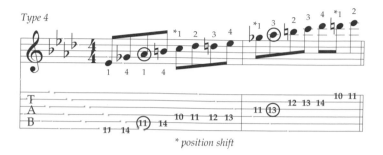

* position shift

Type 5

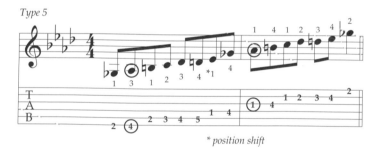

* position shift

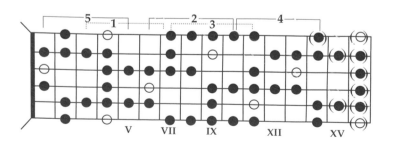

223

A Major (Ionian)

WWHWWWH

Type 1

Type 2

Type 3

Type 4

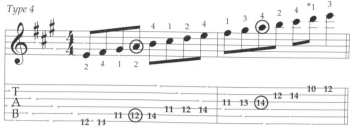

* *position shift*

Type 5

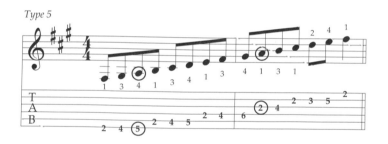

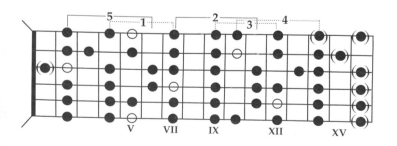

A Natural Minor (Aeolian)

WHWWHWW

Type 1

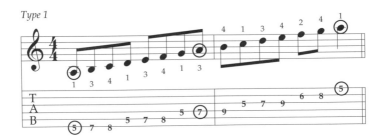

Type 2

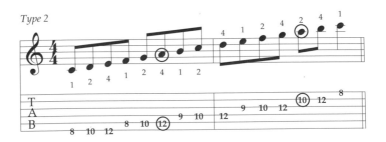

Type 3

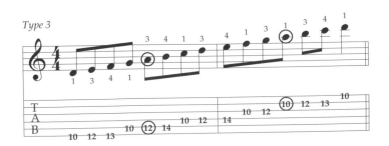

Type 4

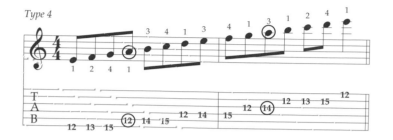

Type 5

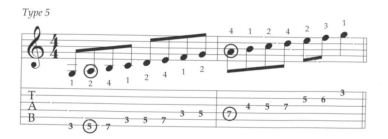

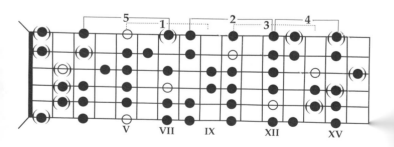

A Dorian

WHWWWHW

Type 1

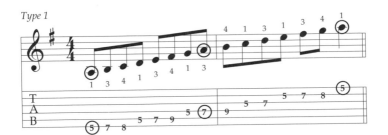

Type 2

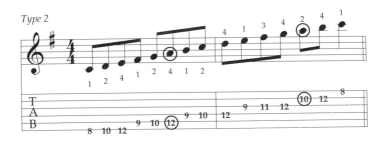

Type 3

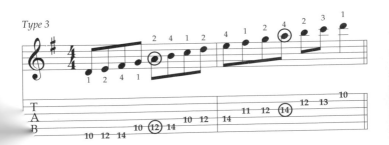

228

Type 4

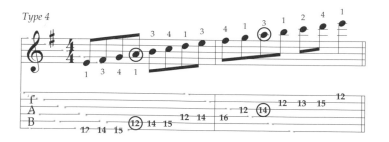

Type 5

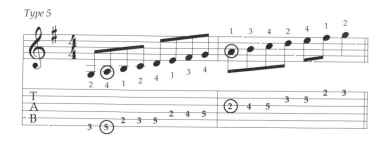

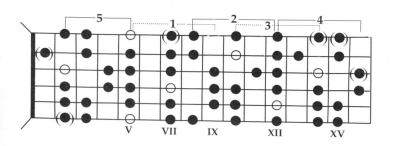

A Phrygian

HWWWHWW

Type 1

Type 2

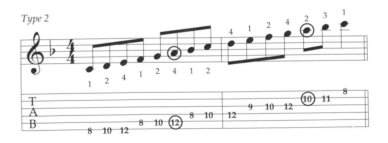

Type 3

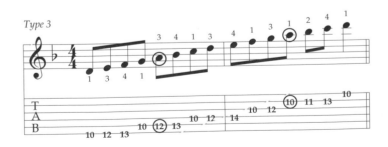

230

Type 4

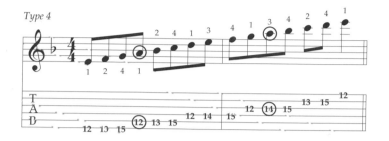

Type 5

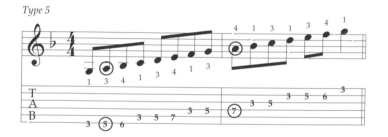

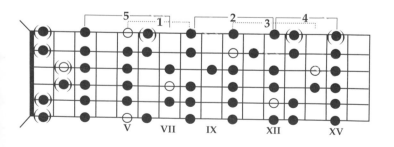

A Lydian

WWWHWWH

Type 1

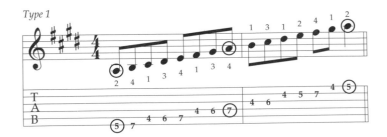

Type 2

Type 3

232

Type 4

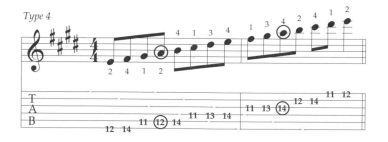

Type 5

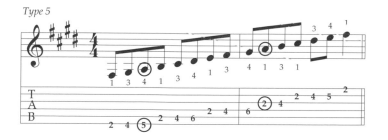

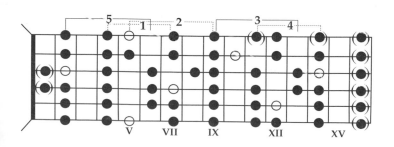

233

A Mixolydian

WWHWWHW

Type 1

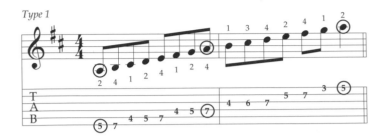

Type 2

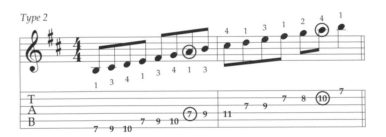

Type 3

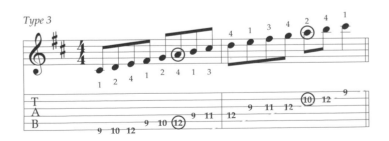

Type 4

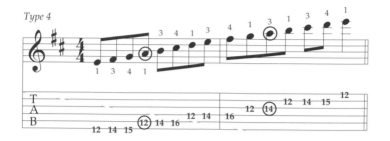

Type 5

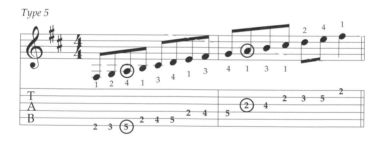

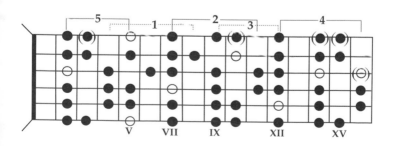

235

A Locrian

HWWHWWW

Type 1

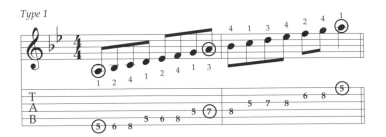

Type 2

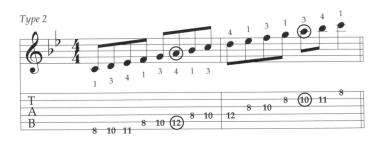

Type 3

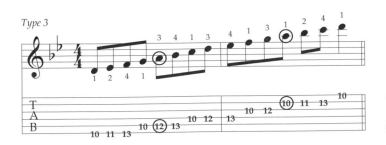

236

Type 4

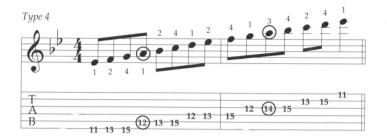

Type 5

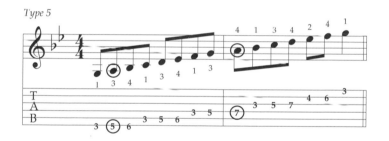

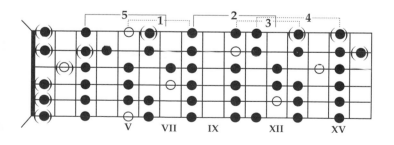

237

A Harmonic Minor

WHWWHm3H

Type 1

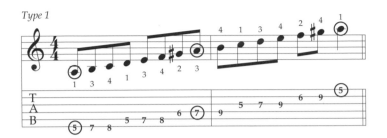

Type 2

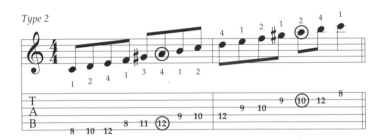

Type 3

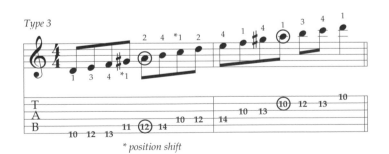

* position shift

Type 4

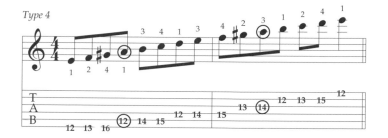

Type 5

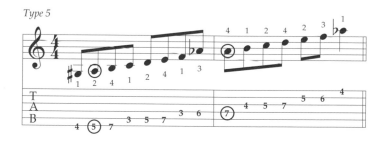

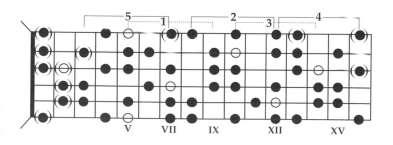

239

A Whole Tone

wwwwww

Type 1

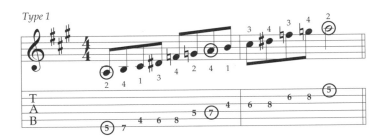

Type 2

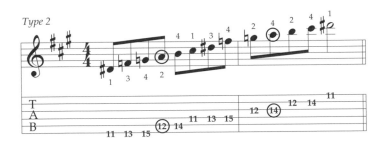

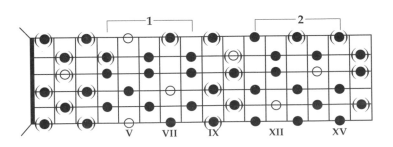

240

A Diminished (whole-half)

WHWHWHWH

Type 1

* position shift

Type 2

* position shift

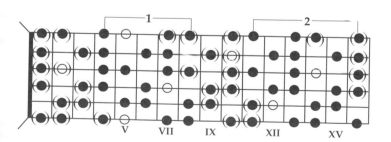

A Pentatonic (Major)

WWm3Wm3

Type 1

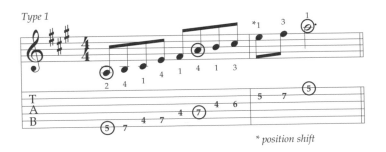

* position shift

Type 2

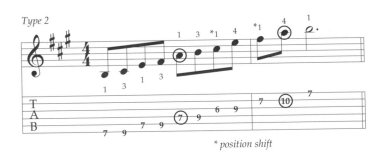

* position shift

Type 3

242

Type 4

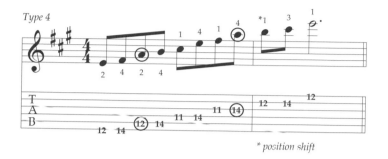

* position shift

Type 5

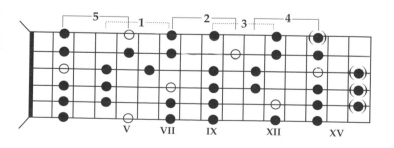

243

A Pentatonic (Minor)

m3WWm3W

Type 1

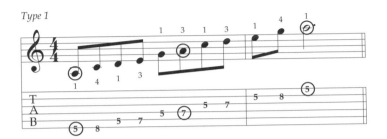

Type 2

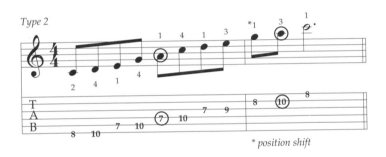

* position shift

Type 3

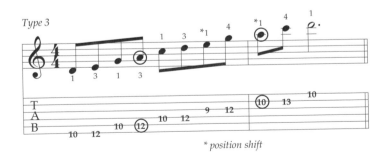

* position shift

Type 4

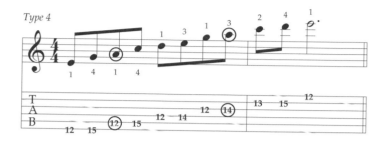

Type 5

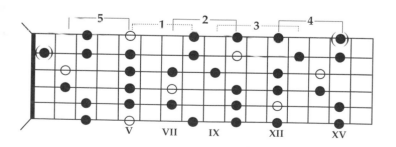

245

A Blues Scale
(with major 3rd & flattened 5th)

m3HHHHm3W

Type 1

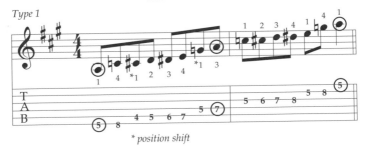

* position shift

Type 2

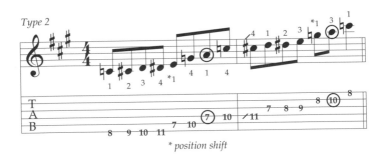

* position shift

Type 3

* position shift

Type 4

position shift

Type 5

position shift

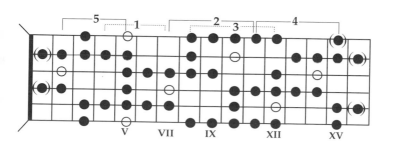

247

B♭ Major (Ionian)

WWHWWWH

Type 1

Type 2

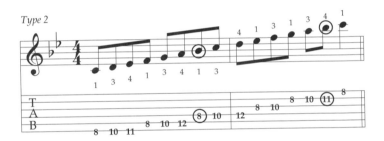

Type 3

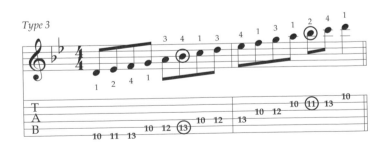

248

Type 4

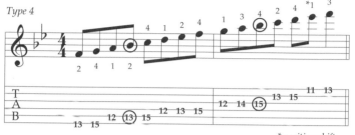

* position shift

Type 5

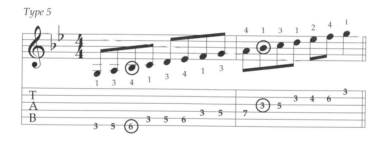

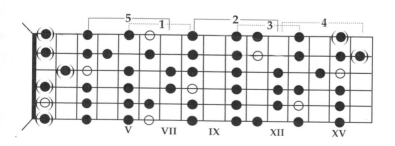

B♭ Natural Minor (Aeolian)

WHWWHWW

Type 1

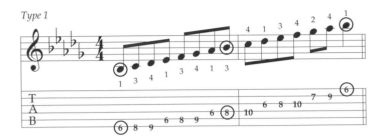

Type 2

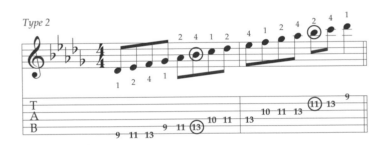

Type 3

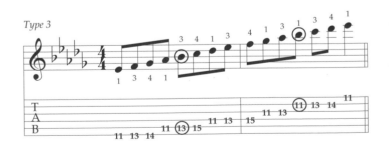

Type 4

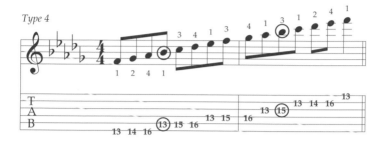

Type 5

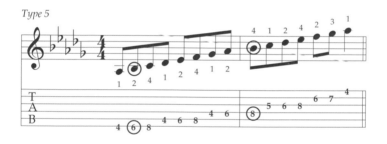

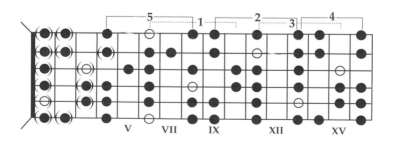

251

B♭ Dorian

WHWWWHW

Type 1

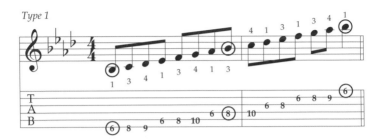

Type 2

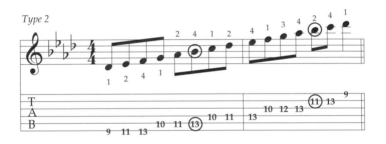

Type 3

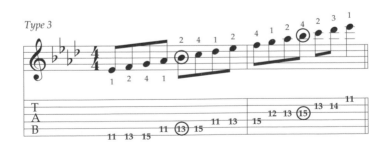

252

Type 4

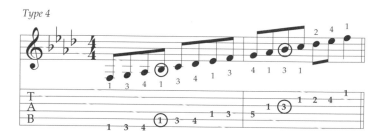

Type 5

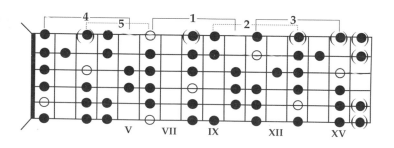

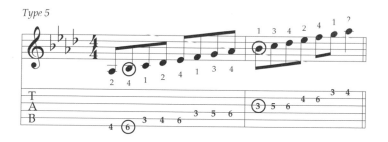

253

B♭ Phrygian

HWWWHWW

Type 1

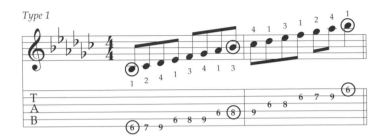

Type 2

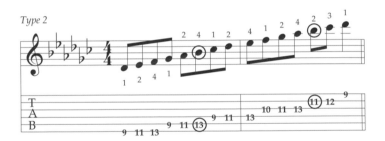

Type 3

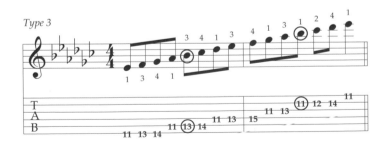

254

Type 4

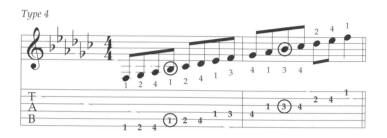

Type 5

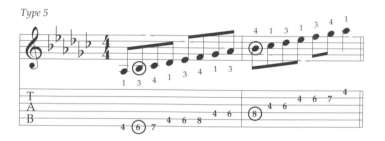

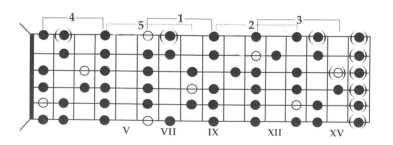

B♭ Lydian

WWWHWWH

Type 1

Type 2

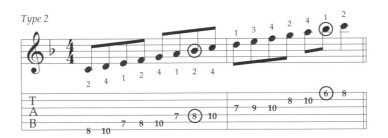

Type 3

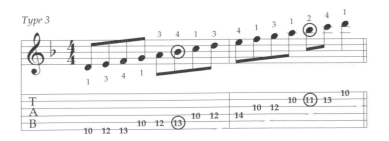

256

Type 4

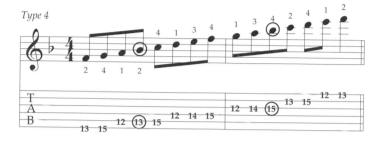

Type 5

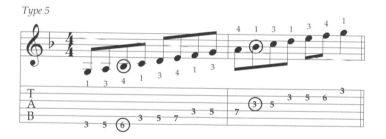

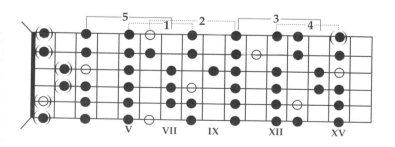

257

B♭ Mixolydian

WWHWWHW

Type 1

Type 2

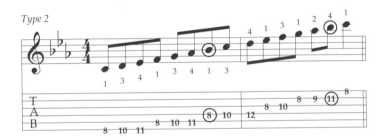

Type 3

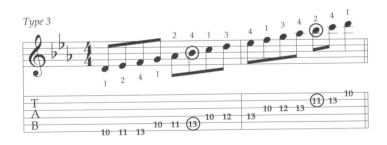

Type 4

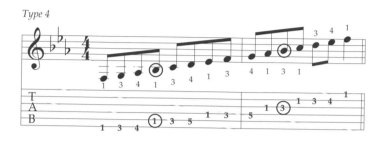

Type 5

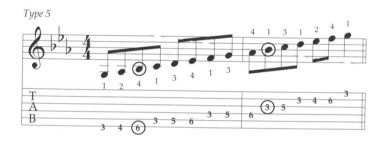

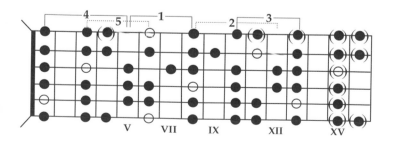

B♭ Locrian

HWWHWWW

Type 1

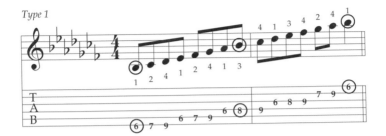

Type 2

Type 3

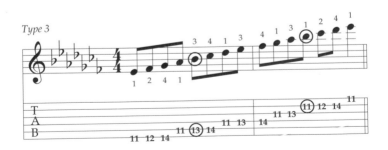

260

Type 4

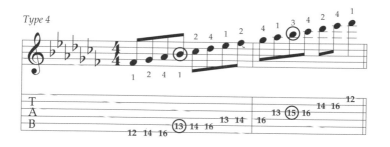

Type 5

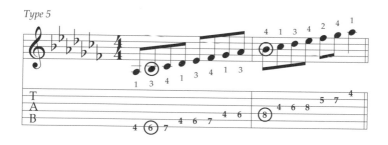

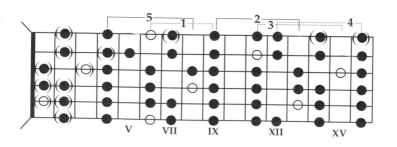

261

B♭ Harmonic Minor

WHWWHm3H

Type 1

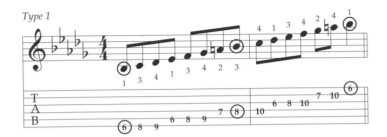

Type 2

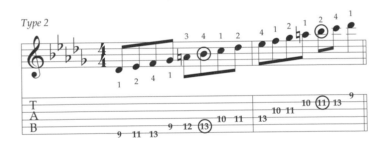

Type 3

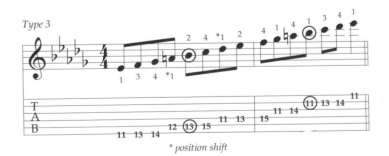

* position shift

262

Type 4

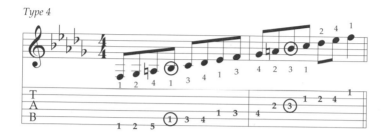

Type 5

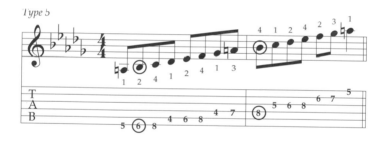

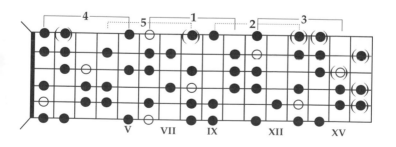

263

B♭ Whole Tone

wwwwww

Type 1

Type 2

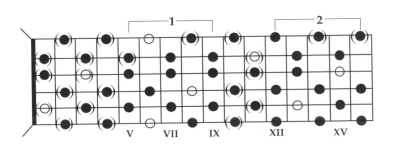

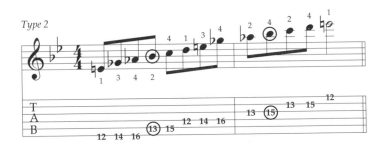

264

B♭ Diminished (whole-half)

WHWHWHWH

Type 1

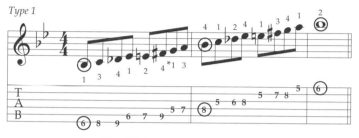

* position shift

Type 2

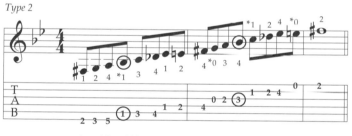

* position shift

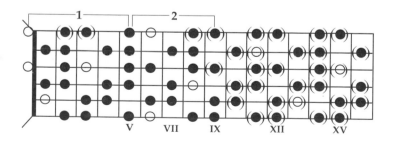

265

B♭ Pentatonic (Major)

WWm3Wm3

Type 1

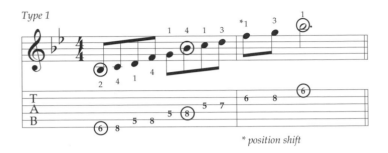

* *position shift*

Type 2

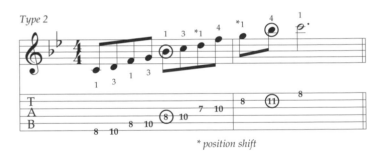

* *position shift*

Type 3

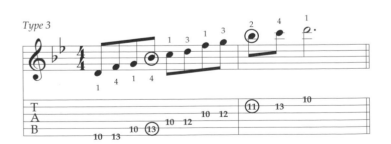

Type 4

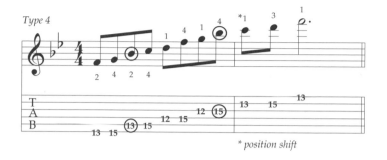

position shift

Type 5

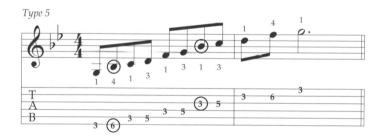

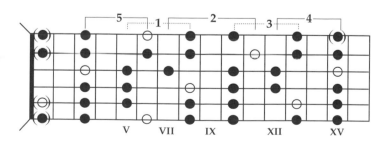

267

B♭ Pentatonic (Minor)

m3WWm3W

Type 1

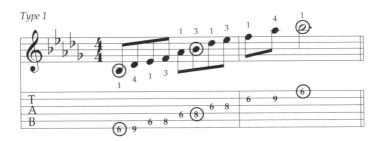

Type 2

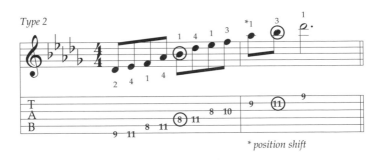

* position shift

Type 3

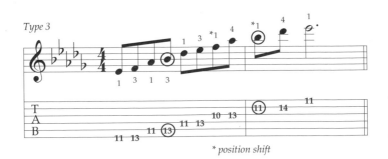

* position shift

Type 4

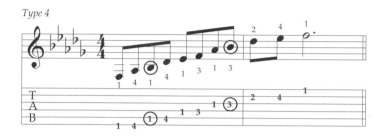

Type 5

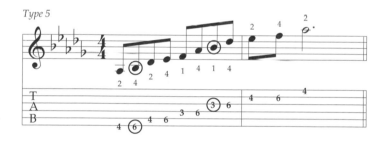

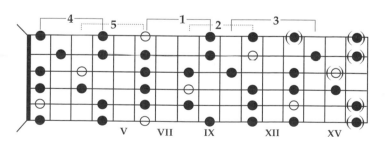

269

B♭ Blues Scale
(with major 3rd & flattened 5th)

m3HHHHm3W

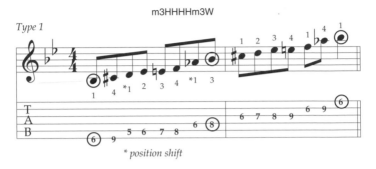

Type 1

* position shift

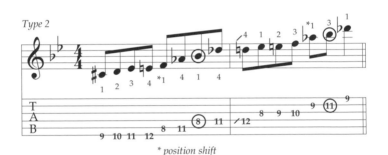

Type 2

* position shift

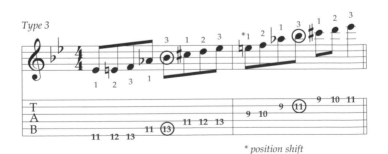

Type 3

* position shift

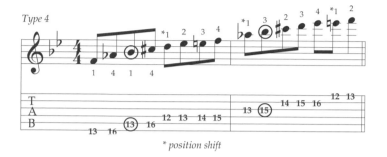

Type 4

* position shift

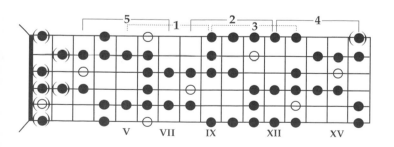

Type 5

* position shift

B Major (Ionian)

WWHWWWH

Type 1

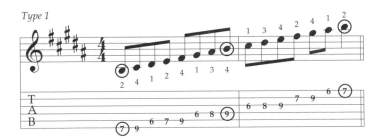

Type 2

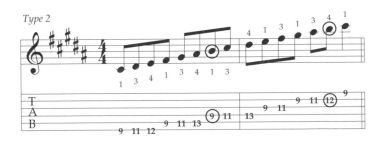

Type 3

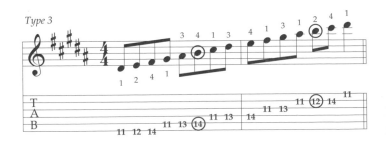

272

Type 4

* position shift

Type 5

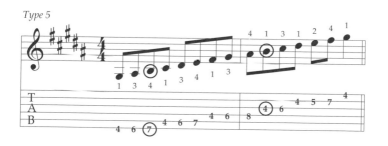

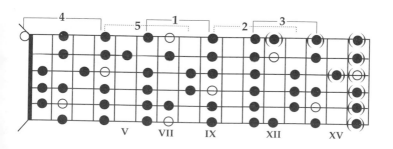

B Natural Minor (Aeolian)

WHWWHWW

Type 1

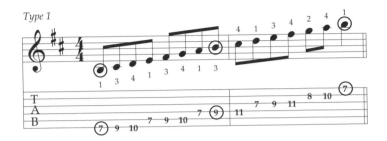

Type 2

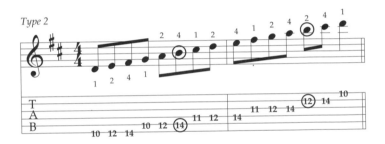

Type 3

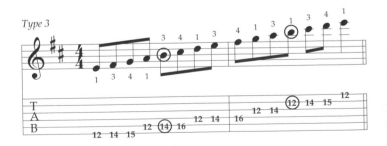

Type 4

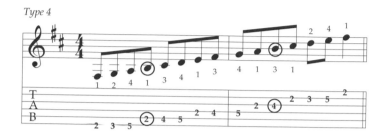

Type 5

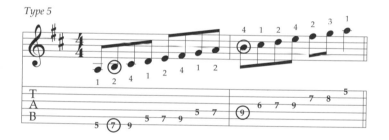

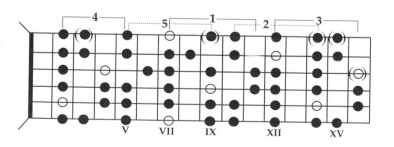

275

B Dorian

WHWWWHW

Type 1

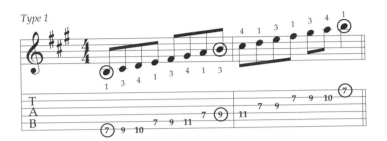

Type 2

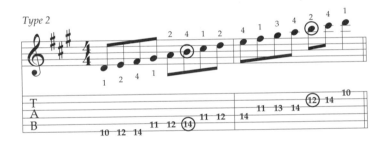

Type 3

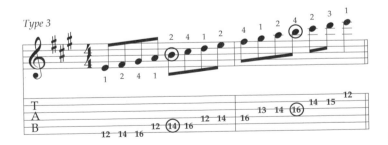

Type 4

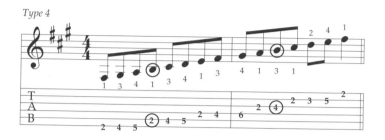

Type 5

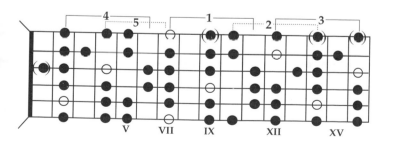

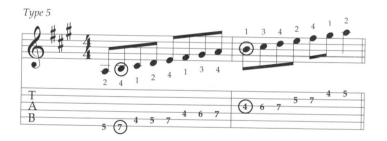

277

B Phrygian

HWWWHWW

Type 1

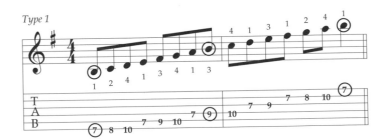

Type 2

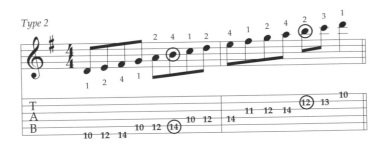

Type 3

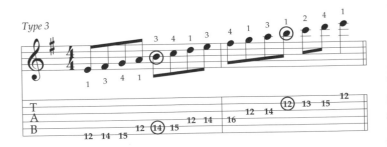

278

Type 4

Type 5

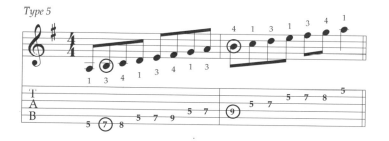

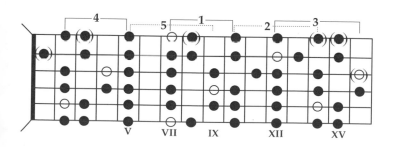

B Lydian

WWWHWWH

Type 1

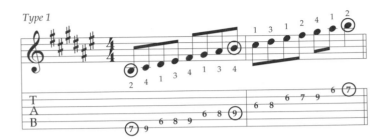

Type 2

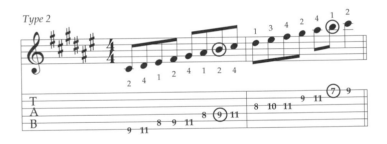

Type 3

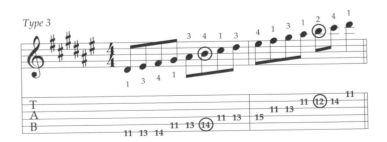

Type 4

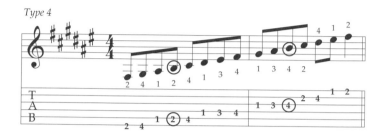

Type 5

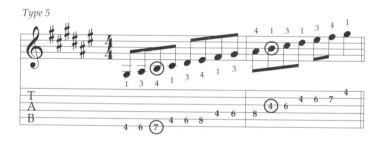

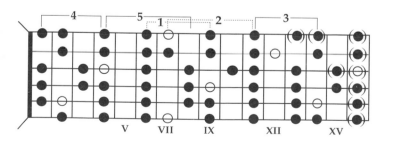

281

B Mixolydian

WWHWWHW

Type 1

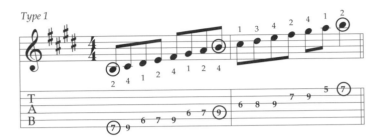

Type 2

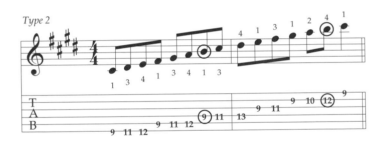

Type 3

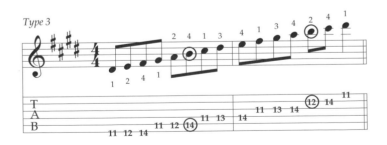

Type 4

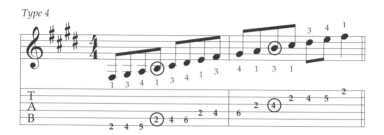

Type 5

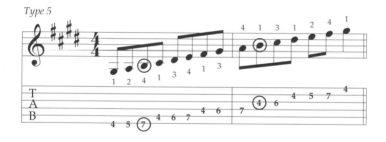

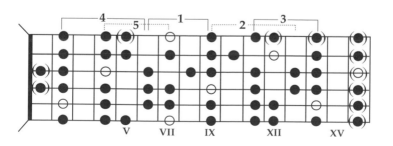

283

B Locrian

HWWHWWW

Type 1

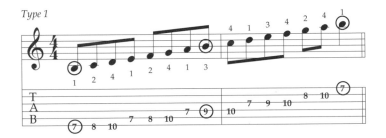

Type 2

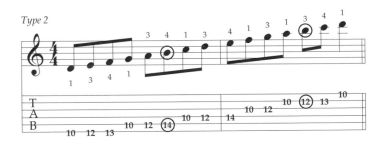

Type 3

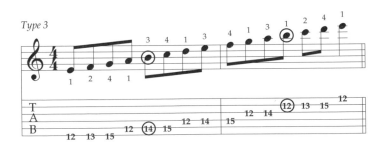

Type 4

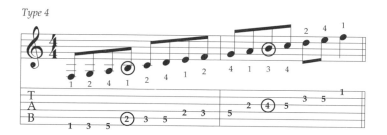

Type 5

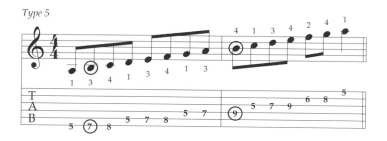

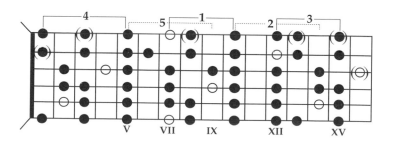

285

B Harmonic Minor

WHWWHm3H

Type 1

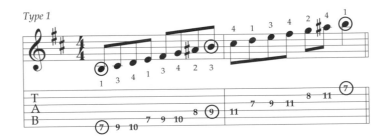

Type 2

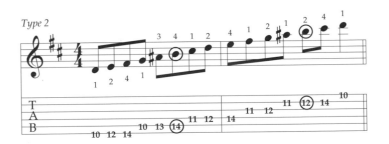

Type 3

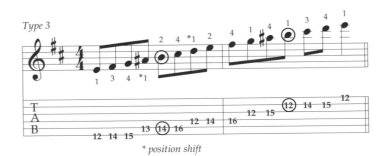

* position shift

286

Type 4

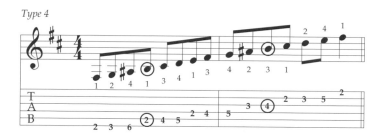

Type 5

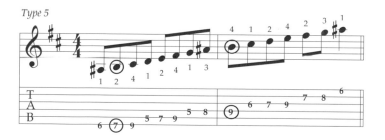

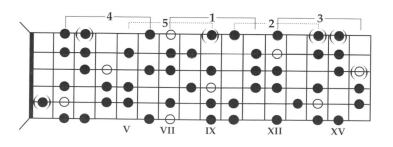

287

B Whole Tone

WWWWWW

Type 1

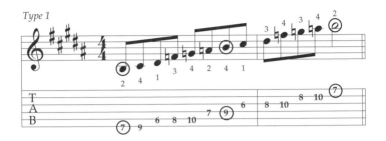

Type 2

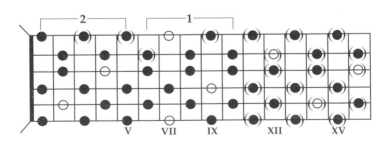

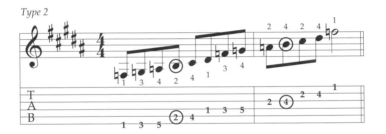

B Diminished (whole-half)

WHWHWHWH

Type 1

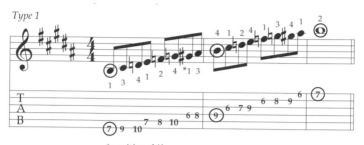

* position shift

Type 2

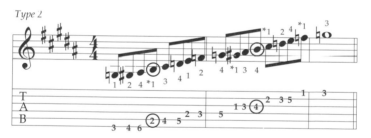

* position shift

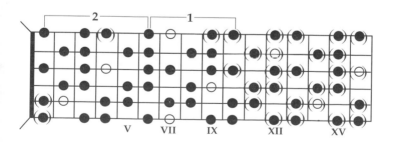

B Pentatonic (Major)

WWm3Wm3

Type 1

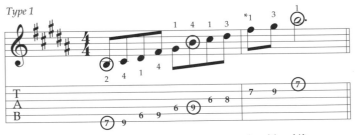

* position shift

Type 2

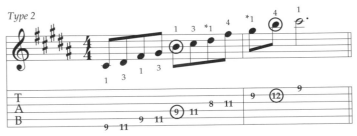

* position shift

Type 3

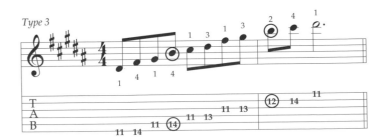

Type 4

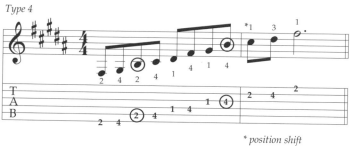

* position shift

Type 5

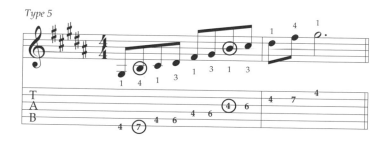

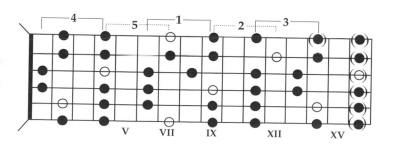

B Pentatonic (Minor)

m3WWm3W

Type 1

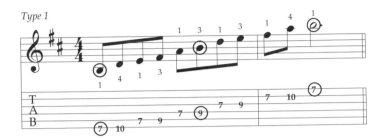

Type 2

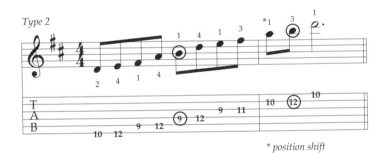

* position shift

Type 3

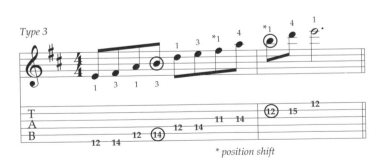

* position shift

Type 4

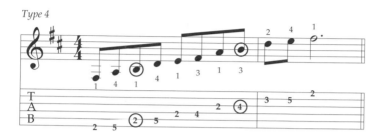

Type 5

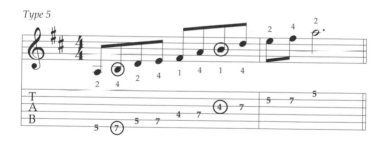

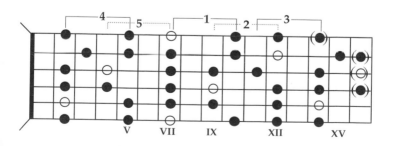

293

B Blues Scale
(with major 3rd & flattened 5th)

m3HHHHm3W

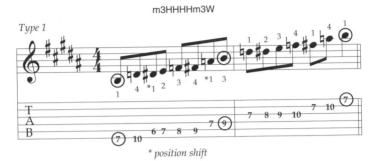

Type 1

* position shift

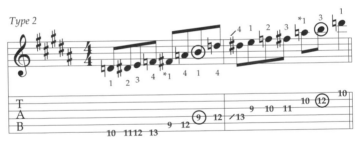

Type 2

* position shift

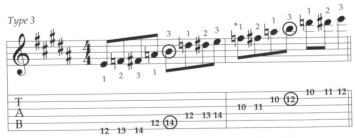

Type 3

* position shift

Type 4

* position shift

Type 5

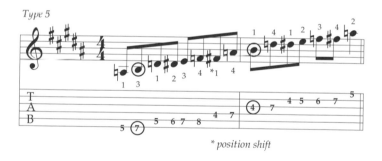

* position shift

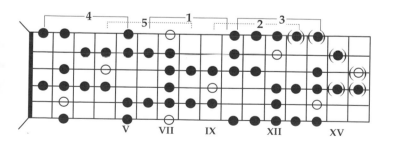

295

Solos and Scales

Learning a new scale isn't the same as learning a new chord – you can't just go and use it straight away. It takes time to get used to its character, and to train your ear to recognise which of the notes work over certain chords. But learning a new scale, or even just a new position for a scale you already know, is a great way of getting your lead playing out of the musical ruts we all find ourselves in from time to time.

Here are some hints and tips on how to turn your hard-learned scales into meaningful solos and riffs. But whatever you want to do with scales, keep this in mind; the most common mistake guitarists make is to play scales far too fast, without really listening to the results.

Do use phrasing. This means playing in musical 'sentences', so the solo can pause at the end of one phrase before it starts the next. Good phrasing gives the listener an opportunity to digest what they've just heard. Remember, the chord backing will carry on while your barrage of notes takes a breather.

Do experiment with timing. Try playing a quick run of four or five short notes, followed by a couple of long, slow ones.

Do use techniques. You can slide up to, or down to, any note of a scale. Try hammer-ons, pull-offs and vibrato to add interest.

Do think like a singer. Once you've played a scale, sing a short musical phrase to yourself, and see if you can figure it out on the guitar.

Do train your ear. Try singing a scale to yourself, then check by playing it back on the guitar to see how familiar you are with its character.

Do play intervals. Why should your solo always go from one note in a scale to the next? Skip a few notes now and again.

Do show off! If you find that a particular pattern of taps, hammer-ons or pull-offs helps you to play a scale pattern more rapidly, go for it!

Do play round the chords. If one note of a scale doesn't sound right over the current chord, try another note from the same scale.

Don't ramble. If you just play up and down the scale at random while the chords cycle past, the audience won't get an idea that there's an interesting guitar melody going on. As a general rule, if you've been playing for more than 4 bars without any rests or long notes, it's time to relax for a couple of beats.

Don't necessarily start solos on the root note. Just because you're playing in F$\sharp$, say, it doesn't mean that the lead part has to begin on that note.

Don't over-use bends. Only a few notes of any scale will sound right when bent. Experiment to find out which these are for each new scale.

Don't use too many effects. The point of learning a new scale is to supply new melodic ideas, so don't blur these with loads of delay and fuzz.

Don't rely too much on 'licks'. These are previously-learned phrases that are played from memory. This will ultimately limit your solos.

Don't play 'scalically' all the time. Running up and down the scale, even at high speed, doesn't always create the most musical result.

Don't try to play too fast. Make sure every note of the scale sounds out cleanly and clearly at a slow tempo before you attempt anything flash.

Don't ignore the chords. If you don't think a note works over a chord, go back and check. Then you won't make the same mistake again.

Don't worry about breaking the rules. If you find a scale that doesn't appear in this book, but you like the way it sounds, use it! You could always write down your scale ideas in the following pages.

"the *little* book... *with all the* SCALES *you'll ever need!*"

13 types of scales in all 12 keys.

A pocket-sized collection of hundreds of scales presented in an easy-to-read format.

Includes fingerings, full TABs for each scale, and helpful tips for all guitarists.

100s
OF
GUITAR
SCALES

8-84088-91843-9

8 84088 91843 9

HL14042424

HAL•LEONARD®

U.S. $12.99

ISBN 978-1-78038-800-7

9 781780 388007

51